D0961076

He who doeth the works
of righteousness
shall receive his reward,
even peace in this world,
and eternal life
in the world to come.

DOCTRINE AND COVENANTS 59:23

FINDING PEACE IN OUR LIVES

JOSEPH B. WIRTHLIN

DESERET BOOK COMPANY
SALT LAKE CITY, UTAH

© 1995 Joseph B. Wirthlin

All rights reserved. No part of this book may be reproduced in any form or by any means without permission in writing from the publisher, Deseret Book Company, P.O. Box 30178, Salt Lake City, Utah 84130. This work is not an official publication of The Church of Jesus Christ of Latter-day Saints. The views expressed herein are the responsibility of the author and do not necessarily represent the position of the Church or of Deseret Book Company.

Deseret Book is a registered trademark of Deseret Book Company.

Library of Congress Cataloging-in-Publication Data

Wirthlin, Joseph B., 1917–
   Finding peace in our lives / Joseph B. Wirthlin
    p.   cm.
   Includes bibliographical references and index.
   ISBN 0-87579-991-4 (hard)
   1. Spiritual life—Mormon Church. 2. Inner peace—Religious aspects—Mormon Church. I. Title.
BX8656.W57   1995
248.4'89332—dc20   95-2234
                                                   CIP

Printed in the United States of America

10 9 8 7 6 5 4 3 2 1

CONTENTS

Contents

PART ONE

Finding Peace with Man and God

Let us therefore follow after the things which make for peace, and things wherewith one may edify another.

ROMANS 14:19

1

PEACE WITHIN

In recent years, peace has been a prominent topic on the minds of people throughout the world, with many countries engaged in war. The news media have shown vivid images of the ravages, suffering, and destruction of war and the turmoil it causes in individuals. It causes deep anxiety and disrupts families, employment, and schooling. It consumes resources that could be used to better advantage elsewhere. Our hearts are filled with compassion for families on all sides who have lost loved ones and for the innocent victims of war, especially children. We pray for a lasting peace when men "shall beat their swords into plowshares, and their spears into pruninghooks: . . . neither shall they learn war any more." (Isaiah 2:4.)

In the scriptures, *peace* means either freedom from strife, contention, conflict, or war, or an inner calm and comfort born of the Spirit that is a gift of God to all of his children, an assurance and serenity within a person's heart. One dictionary has defined peace as a state of tranquillity or quiet, freedom from disquieting thoughts or emotions, and harmony in personal relations.[1]

While we yearn for peace, we live in a world burdened with hunger, pain, anguish, loneliness, sickness, and sorrow. We see divorce with its attendant conflict and heartache, especially among the innocent children caught in the middle. Wayward, disobedient children cause their parents grief and anxiety. Financial problems cause distress and loss of self-respect. Some loved ones slip into sin and wickedness, forsake their covenants, and walk in their "own way, and after the image of [their] own god." (D&C 1:16.)

The value of peace within our hearts cannot be measured. When we are at peace, we can be free of worry and fear, knowing that with the Lord's help, we can do all that is expected or required of us. We can approach every day, every task, and every challenge with assurance and confidence in the outcome. We have freedom of thought and action, freedom to be happy. Even those who might be incarcerated for lengthy periods as war prisoners can be at peace in their own minds. Many of them learn that their captors cannot deprive them of freedom to think, even when the harshest limitations are imposed. Few, if any, blessings from God are more valuable to our spiritual health than the reward of peace within. In modern-day revelation the Savior said, "He who doeth the works of righteousness shall receive his reward, even peace in this world, and eternal life in the world to come." (D&C 59:23.)

Despite dismal conditions in the world and the personal challenges that come into every life, peace within can be a reality. We can be calm and serene regardless of the swirling turmoil all about us. Attaining harmony within ourselves depends upon our relationship with our Savior and Redeemer, Jesus Christ, and our willingness to emulate him by living the principles he has given us. He has extended to us an invitation: "Come unto me, all ye that labour and are heavy laden, and I will give you rest. Take my yoke upon you, and learn of me; for I am meek and lowly in heart: and ye shall find rest

4

unto your souls. For my yoke is easy, and my burden is light."
(Matthew 11:28–30.)

The phrase "Peace, be still" (Mark 4:39), which the Savior
uttered when he calmed the storm-tossed sea, can have the
same calming influence upon us when we are buffeted by
life's storms. During the Passover feast, the Savior taught his
disciples: "Peace I leave with you, my peace I give unto you:
not as the world giveth, give I unto you. Let not your heart
be troubled, neither let it be afraid." (John 14:27.) Referring
to the teachings he had given to his disciples, Jesus said:
"These things I have spoken unto you, that in me ye might
have peace. In the world ye shall have tribulation: but be of
good cheer; I have overcome the world." (John 16:33.)

In his epistle to the Romans, Paul gave us one key to finding the peace promised by the Lord: "To be spiritually minded
is life and peace." (Romans 8:6.)

One faithful mother of a large family learned to find peace
by accepting the Savior's invitation to come unto him and
find rest. She lived in obedience to the commandments of
God and had faith in the Lord, Jesus Christ. She developed
the practice of doing everything within her power to solve
problems and meet challenges, and then, when she felt that
she could do nothing more, she would cast her burdens upon
the Lord and place the outcome in his hands.

President David O. McKay said, "The peace of Christ does
not come by seeking the superficial things of life, neither does
it come except as it springs from the individual's heart." He
said further that this peace is "conditioned upon obedience
to the principles of the Gospel of Jesus Christ. . . . No man
is at peace with himself or his God who is untrue to his
better self, who transgresses the law of right either in dealing
with himself by indulging in passion, in appetite, yielding to

5

temptations against his accusing conscience, or in dealing with his fellowmen, being untrue to their trust. Peace does not come to the transgressor of law; peace comes by obedience to law, and it is that message which Jesus would have us proclaim among men."[2]

Earth life is a period of probation, to provide an opportunity for choices. Two mighty forces are pulling in opposite directions. On the one hand we find the power of Christ and his righteousness. On the other hand are Satan and the spirits who follow him. President Marion G. Romney said: "Mankind . . . must determine to travel in company with the one or the other. The reward for following the one is the fruit of the Spirit—peace. The reward for following the other is the works of the flesh—the antithesis of peace." Further, he said: "The price of peace is victory over Satan."[3] We can know which one to follow because God has given us the Spirit of Christ to know good from evil and to protect ourselves from sin. (See Moroni 7:15–18.)

The Spirit of Christ and the Holy Ghost give direction based on obedience. This direction can lead to repentance and a change in attitude and behavior. Conscience is a feeling of right or wrong based on our cultural, moral, and religious background. Conscience can be rationalized by social circumstance while the Spirit of Christ and the Holy Ghost will direct our conduct in the paths of righteousness continuously in all circumstances.

If we follow the promptings of the Spirit of Christ, we can be free of sin and filled with peace. If we do not, but instead let our carnal appetites control us, we never will know true peace. We will be tossed "like the troubled sea, when it cannot rest. . . . There is no peace, saith . . . God, to the wicked." (Isaiah 57:20–21.) If we ignore these promptings, we can lose that gift because we no longer are sensitive to it. We will be beyond feeling, beyond the influence of that Spirit. (See 1 Nephi 17:45; Ephesians 4:19.)

Though we abhor war, peace nearly always is more a dream than a reality. During most of the world's history, strife, dissension, and conflict have flourished and displaced peace. The times when peace has reigned, it has begun in the hearts of righteous, obedient individuals and has grown until it has engulfed a society. We have scriptural accounts of at least two periods of absolute peace, and a third that is yet to come.

The first of these periods of peace was among the people of Enoch, who lived before the great flood. They continued in righteousness, and "the Lord came and dwelt with" them. He "called his people Zion, because they were of one heart and one mind, and dwelt in righteousness." They "built a city that was called the City of Holiness, even Zion," which, in the "process of time, was taken up into heaven." (Moses 7:16–21.)

The second period of peace followed the ministry of the resurrected Jesus among the Nephites. They abolished the works of evil and obtained the fruit of the Spirit. In the Book of Mormon we read: "The disciples of Jesus had formed a church of Christ. . . . And as many as did come unto them, and did truly repent of their sins, were baptized in the name of Jesus; and they did also receive the Holy Ghost." Consequently, "there were no contentions and disputations among them, and every man did deal justly one with another . . . because of the love of God which did dwell in the hearts of the people. And there were no envyings, nor strifes, nor tumults, nor whoredoms, nor lyings, nor murders, nor any manner of lasciviousness. . . . And surely there could not be a happier people among all the people who had been created

7

by the hand of God," for "they were in one, the children of Christ, and heirs to the kingdom of God." (4 Nephi 1:1–2, 15–17.)

Peace prevailed among the Nephites for almost two centuries. Then some of them deserted the teachings of Jesus Christ and turned to selfish pride and wickedness. Within another two centuries, the Nephite nation that had enjoyed this long period of perfect peace had destroyed itself in savage civil war.

A third period of perfect peace will come during the Millennium, a time when "Satan shall be bound, that he shall have no place in the hearts of the children of men." (D&C 45:55.) As they live the gospel of Jesus Christ, the righteous people will banish Satan from their midst. We look forward to that day of universal peace and justice, when Christ will reign upon the earth.

These three instances show that peace, whether in a city, a nation, or another society, develops from peace that begins within the hearts of individuals as they live by the precepts of the gospel.

We see an example of individual peace amidst strife and contention in the life of the Prophet Joseph Smith. Near the end of his life, he was at the center of a whirlwind of turmoil and tribulation caused by devious associates, false accusations, and cunning plots against his life. Yet a few days before his death, he said, "I am calm as a summer's morning; I have a conscience void of offense towards God, and towards all men." (D&C 135:4.) His inner peace sustained him through monumental adversities, even his own martyrdom.

Peace is more than a lofty ideal. It is a practical principle that, with conscious effort, can become a normal part of our lives as we deal with matters both large and small. One habit that prevents inner peace is procrastination. It clutters our minds with unfinished business and makes us uneasy until we finish a task and get it out of the way. We are at peace in our church callings when we do the work at the proper time instead of waiting until the last possible moment. This is true of going to the temple often, performing our home teaching and visiting teaching assignments, preparing lessons and talks, and doing other assignments.

Can anyone's mind be at peace if he or she is unfaithful in even the least degree to marriage vows? How much mental anguish results from a little lying, cheating, or stealing, even if they are never discovered? Do we have peace of mind if we knowingly violate traffic laws? Or do we watch nervously for the ever-present policeman? Do we have peace of mind if we are not honest with our employers and do not give fair value for the pay we receive? Are we at peace if we are less than honest regarding our tax returns?

Latter-day Saints are obligated to seek inner peace not only for the blessing it is to them but also so that they can radiate its influence to others. In a Christmas message, the First Presidency proclaimed that the Church has a divine commission to establish peace. Church members are to "manifest brotherly love, first toward one another, then toward all mankind; to seek unity, harmony and peace . . . within the Church, and then, by precept and example, extend these virtues throughout the world."[4]

If sin has deprived us of peace within, we can repent and seek forgiveness. The Lord said that he "cannot look upon sin with the least degree of allowance; nevertheless, he that repents and does the commandments of the Lord shall be forgiven." (D&C 1:31–32.) President Spencer W. Kimball wrote: "The essence of the miracle of forgiveness is that it brings peace to the previously anxious, restless, frustrated, perhaps tormented soul. In a world of turmoil and contention this is indeed a priceless gift."[5]

We *can* be at peace if we "let virtue garnish [our] thoughts unceasingly." (D&C 121:45.) The power is in us as spirit children of our Heavenly Father. He and his Beloved Son, Jesus Christ, have provided the way for us to be at peace. We *can* enjoy that peace of God which passeth human understanding. (See Philippians 4:7.) We can enjoy it personally, within our families, in our communities, in our nations, and in our world if we will do the things that produce it. This peace leads to happiness.

NOTES

1. *Webster's Tenth New Collegiate Dictionary* (Springfield, Massachusetts: Merriam Webster, Inc., 1993), p. 854.
2. Conference Report, October 1938, p. 133.
3. See Marion G. Romney, "The Price of Peace," *Ensign*, October 1983, pp. 3–7.
4. "Greetings from the First Presidency," *Liahona, the Elders' Journal*, December 22, 1936, p. 315.
5. Spencer W. Kimball, *The Miracle of Forgiveness* (Salt Lake City: Bookcraft, 1969), p. 363.

2

THE LORD'S SIDE

One of the great hymns of the Restoration is "Who's on the Lord's Side?" written by Hannah Last Cornaby, an English convert to the Church, born in 1822. The words of this hymn seem particularly attuned to our time and society. The hymn impressed me when I was a small boy in the Salt Lake City Thirty-third Ward. It apparently was our Sunday School chorister's favorite song; we seemed to sing it every Sunday. We young children would leave Sunday School singing "Who's on the Lord's side? Who? Now is the time to show." The words and melody would stay in our minds after we sang it. In fact, I've never forgotten it or our chorister.

The words of the hymn echo the words of Moses as he called the rebellious children of Israel to repentance after he had destroyed the idolatrous calf they had made. "Then Moses stood in the gate of the camp, and said, Who is on the Lord's side? let him come unto me. . . . Consecrate yourselves to day to the Lord." (Exodus 32:26, 29.)

Joshua, who succeeded Moses, told the children of Israel essentially the same thing after he had led them into their promised land of Canaan. Shortly before his death, he called the people of Israel together for a final blessing and warning, much as Moses had done. What a prophet says as he nears the end of his life is very important, because he is concluding his accountability and placing the full responsibility on the shoulders of others for their own conduct. Joshua reviewed with Israel exactly what God had miraculously done for them and then exhorted them:

"Choose ye this day whom ye will serve; whether the gods which your fathers served that were on the other side of the flood, or the gods of the Amorites, in whose land ye dwell: but as for me and my house, we will serve the Lord. . . . And the people said unto Joshua, The Lord our God will we serve, and his voice will we obey." (Joshua 24:15, 24.)

We too must choose whether we will serve our Lord and Savior, Jesus Christ, or follow the gods of indulgence and sin that clamor for our attention on every side.

The Lord has left no doubt in defining his side and where the Saints should be in their thoughts, words, actions, and practices. We have his counsel in the scriptures and in the words of the prophets. To ancient Israel, the Lord said through Moses: "I have set before thee this day life and good, and death and evil." (Deuteronomy 30:15.) The Lord counseled his prophet Jeremiah to instruct the people on the way of life, and the way of death. (Jeremiah 21:8.) That is the contrast; that is the choice. Either we are on the Lord's side of the line or on the side of the adversary. As Nephi declared, we "are free to act" for ourselves—"to choose the way of everlasting death or the way of eternal life." (2 Nephi 10:23.)

Yes, "men are free according to the flesh; and all things are given them which are expedient unto man. And they are free to choose liberty and eternal life, through the great Mediator of all men, or to choose captivity and death, according to the captivity and power of the devil; for he seeketh that all men might be miserable like unto himself." (2 Nephi 2:27.)

The line between those who are on the Lord's side and

12

those who follow the adversary has been with us from the beginning. Even before the creation of this world, the children of God divided themselves into two groups with different loyalties. One-third of the host of heaven followed Lucifer, separating themselves from the presence of God and from the two-thirds who followed the Son of God. (See D&C 29:36–39.)

This division has persisted throughout the history of mankind and will continue until the day of judgment when Jesus comes again in his glory. We read in Matthew that all nations will gather before him, and he will "separate them one from another, as a shepherd divideth his sheep from the goats: and he shall set the sheep on his right hand, but the goats on the left.

"Then shall the King say unto them on his right hand, Come, ye blessed of my Father, inherit the kingdom prepared for you from the foundation of the world. . . .

"Then shall he say also unto them on the left hand, Depart from me, ye cursed, into everlasting fire, prepared for the devil and his angels." (Matthew 25:32–34, 41.)

The prophet Nephi tells us why many choose the wrong side of the line: "Now the cause of this iniquity of the people was this—Satan had great power, unto the stirring up of the people to do all manner of iniquity, and to the puffing them up with pride, tempting them to seek for power, and authority, and riches, and the vain things of the world." (3 Nephi 6:15.)

The Lord has given us prophets to guide us and keep us from evil if we will accept and follow their instruction. The Lord would say to us today as he said to the ancient Israelites: "Be not afraid nor dismayed . . . for the battle is not yours, but God's. . . . Believe in the Lord your God, so shall ye

13

be established; believe the prophets, so shall ye prosper." (2 Chronicles 20:15, 20.)

In our conferences, we sustain the First Presidency and the Twelve Apostles as prophets, seers, and revelators. The Lord has appointed them as watchmen to warn the people (see Ezekiel 2:1–8; 33:6–7) and as the "servant[s] of all" (D&C 50:26). He declared, "Whether by mine own voice or by the voice of my servants, it is the same." (D&C 1:38.)

One latter-day prophet, President George Albert Smith, said: "The spirit of the adversary is the spirit of destruction. There are two influences in the world. The one is the influence of our Heavenly Father and the other is the influence of Satan. We can take our choice which territory we want to live in, that of our Heavenly Father or that of Satan." President Smith then quoted his grandfather, who said, "There is a line of demarcation, well defined. On one side of the line is the Lord's territory. On the other side of the line is the devil's territory. . . . If you will stay on the Lord's side of the line, you are perfectly safe, because the adversary of all righteousness can not cross that line."

"What does that mean?" President Smith asked. "It means to me that those who are living righteous lives, keeping all of the commandments of our Heavenly Father are perfectly safe, but not those who trifle with his advice and counsel."[1]

Other latter-day prophets have issued warnings, when inspired by the Lord, on such subjects as moral cleanliness, Sabbath observance, child and spouse abuse, homosexuality, abortion, and gambling. These statements are the word of the Lord through his prophets to help people avoid the pitfalls, sorrow, suffering, and misery of sin and error.

The statements of the prophets are not given to compel, coerce, dictate, or control us, or infringe on any person's right to choose. Church leaders are guided by the Lord's injunction in the Doctrine and Covenants: "No power or influence can or ought to be maintained by virtue of the priesthood, only by persuasion, by long-suffering, by gentleness and meekness, and by love unfeigned; by kindness, and pure knowledge, which shall greatly enlarge the soul without hypocrisy, and without guile." (D&C 121:41–42.)

The prophets and other Church leaders have never misled the Latter-day Saints on a principle of righteousness. Every principle is for our benefit. However, if we choose to ignore the prophets, we choose the consequences that follow. We have the God-given agency to either follow the prophets or not, but we cannot choose the consequences of exercising that agency. They will follow with absolute certainty. If we ignore the prophets, we become like the people the Savior chastised when he said, "Why call ye me, Lord, Lord, and do not the things which I say?" (Luke 6:46.)

In addition to the scriptures and the words of modern-day prophets, the promptings of the Spirit can help Latter-day Saints to discern clearly what they must do to be on the Lord's side.

To be on the Lord's side, we need to learn that true principles will lead us to peace and happiness in this world, and to glory and exaltation in the world to come. We also need to learn that choosing the other side will only bring us problems, heartache, and sorrow. If we come too close to the line and tarry too long in the presence of evil, we are asking for trouble, because we increase the likelihood that we might slip over the line into the territory of the adversary and become supporters of his cause instead of the Lord's.

We must be cautious of seemingly small thoughts and actions that can lead to large consequences. Just a little anger, unkindness, or disobedience; a dishonest deed; a few unclean thoughts; a little pornography; one experiment with drugs; a few lies; a little fraud; or a feeling of hate can lead us into the camp of the adversary. Giving just an inch here and there can put us close enough to the line that one slip will take us right over it. Those who decide to experiment with only one cigarette, one dose of drugs, or one drink of alcohol—only one—often find themselves led into additional use, and in time they become addicted to a substance that controls them, an addiction that they can break only with great difficulty.

Men and women who decide to flirt with adultery just once can become enmeshed in misery and unhappiness for themselves and their precious families. Few are able to get back on the Lord's side immediately. Too many lose a loving companion, face separation from their children, develop bitterness, lose their economic stability, and lose their eternal blessings unless they repent.

The Church has only one acceptable standard of sexual morality: complete chastity for both sexes. I urge you to avoid situations that permit physical feelings to take control of behavior. The notion that a person can endanger his or her physical and mental health by letting strong passions go unsatisfied is a vicious falsehood. Self-control is one mark of a mature person; it applies to control of language, physical treatment of others, and the appetites of the body.

The Lord said, "Remember the sabbath day, to keep it holy" (Exodus 20:8), and made Sabbath day observance a sign between him and the people to indicate their obedience (see Exodus 31:13–17). That commandment and that sign have never been rescinded.

In our day, standards for keeping the Sabbath day holy are lowered a little at a time by some individuals until practically anything seems to become acceptable. The sign between the Lord and his covenant people is trampled underfoot as Latter-day Saints skip Sunday meetings to seek recreation at lakes and beaches, in the mountains, at sports arenas, and at theaters. Parking lots at supermarkets and discount stores often are full on Sundays. Many store owners feel compelled to open their doors on Sundays because of the demand for the merchandise and services. The people who misuse the Sabbath lose the blessings of spiritual food and growth promised to those who keep this commandment.

If we are to be on the Lord's side, we must be very careful of the entertainment media we allow into our homes. Parents sometimes allow their children to see and hear things that are objectionable because they have difficulty finding a movie, videotape, or television program that does not contain offensive elements. Rather than ban such entertainment, many parents permit their children to watch a movie with violence or profanity or sexual content, hoping their children will realize that Hollywood's standards do not reflect those of the parents.

The difference between Hollywood's standards and the standards of most Americans is appalling, as shown in a recent study: "More than one hundred top television writers and executives were asked questions that paralleled a poll taken of average American viewers. The results:

"A whopping 85 percent of the country believes adultery to be wrong. But in Hollywood, it's 49 percent.

"A minute 4 percent of the nation says it has no religious affiliation, compared to 45 percent in Hollywood.

"Some 76 percent of Americans feel [homosexuality is] wrong. In Hollywood, it's 20 percent.

"Abortion rights are supported by 59 percent of the

country [which is appalling] compared to Hollywood's 97 percent."[2]

Truly, parents and children need to be diligent and cautious in choosing what types of entertainment to take into their homes.

Now is the time to show which side of the line we are on. Alma said, "This life is the time for men to prepare to meet God." (Alma 34:32.) We may need courage to take a stand. We may be unpopular. There may be some groups and associates who disregard our standards and even scoff at our ideals and beliefs.

Isn't it interesting that many people consider it "freedom of expression" to profane the Lord's name and use obscenities, yet they oppose prayer in public places. Some people combat public faith and prayer, yet uphold the right of anyone to have an abortion. And some openly oppose good and promote evil.

Being on the Lord's side means not only that we shun evil but also that we seek and cultivate good wherever it can be found, whether within or outside the Church. In a general conference address, President Howard W. Hunter declared:

"As members of the Church of Jesus Christ, we seek to bring all truth together. We seek to enlarge the circle of love and understanding among all the people of the earth. Thus we strive to establish peace and happiness, not only within Christianity but among all mankind.

"In the message of the gospel, the entire human race is one family descended from a single God. . . . Every person is a spiritual child of God. In this gospel view there is no room for a contracted, narrow, or prejudicial view. . . . There is no underlying excuse for smugness, arrogance, or pride. . . .

"We believe there is a spiritual influence that emanates

from the presence of God to fill the immensity of space. (See D&C 88:12.) All men share an inheritance of divine light. God operates among his children in all nations, and those who seek God are entitled to further light and knowledge, regardless of their race, nationality, or cultural traditions.

"Elder Orson F. Whitney . . . explained that . . . '[God] is using not only his covenant people, but other peoples as well, to consummate a work, stupendous, magnificent, and altogether too arduous for this little handful of Saints to accomplish by and of themselves.'"[3]

Recognizing this broad view of who can do good, we must be cautious that we do not confuse opposition to wrong-headed ideas or dangerous practices with opposition to sincere, good-hearted people. Many good and honest people of different faiths or of no faith at all are on the Lord's side in seeking the betterment of their fellowmen and exerting a positive influence on society. Please consider with me a few examples of such good people.

A national magazine recently included a feature article about two brothers, not Latter-day Saints but with Utah roots, whose acts of kindness are on the Lord's side. They honor people who are committed to serving others. Since 1988, Val and Bill Halamandaris have given the National Caring Awards in Washington, D.C. Recipients have included both famous and obscure adults and young people, such as a former U.S. Secretary of Health, Education, and Welfare; a lifelong resident of Watts in the Los Angeles area who has single-handedly found housing for hundreds of homeless neighbors; a world-famous physician; and a Minneapolis housewife who on her own established a soup kitchen.

Successful in their business and government careers, the two brothers were "concerned with the materialism of the country and the tremendous amount of attention we were paying to celebrities. There are millions of people doing extraordinary things in this country, and nobody was honoring them.

"How did two brothers in their late forties, with successful careers in Washington, come to devote so much of their lives to an ideal as abstract—and certainly unremunerative—as caring?" the writer of the article asks. "As it turned out, the story began long ago.

"'We're a couple of kids from Carbon County, Utah,' Val explained. 'After the railroad met at Promontory in 1869, they shipped a lot of the railroad workers—Chinese, Greeks, Italians—down to Carbon County to work in the coal mines. Our grandfather was a Greek immigrant who worked on the railroads. Our father was a miner. We grew up in a multicultural society where everybody was comfortable with everybody else, where we were constantly reminded of the goodness of people. We heard about the importance of doing things for others day in and day out.' As Bill remembered: 'When somebody needed something, you did what had to be done. . . . There is joy in transcending yourself to serve others.'"4

These brothers are good people who are honoring those who care for and serve others. Their efforts are the fruits of having learned in their youth to accept those who are different from themselves, not judging wrongly but simply serving.

Others who are on the Lord's side are the gifted authors and composers whose inspired and sacred hymns convey deep spiritual messages in meetings of congregations in many parts of the world, enriching our church and many others.

Just three months after the Church was organized in 1830, the Lord commanded Emma Smith, the Prophet Joseph's wife, to "make a selection of sacred hymns . . . to be had in my church. For," he explained, "my soul delighteth in the song of the heart; yea, the song of the righteous is a prayer unto me, and it shall be answered with a blessing upon their heads." (D&C 25:11–12.)

In the preface to the 1985 LDS hymnal, the First Presidency wrote that "inspirational music is an essential part of our church meetings. The hymns invite the Spirit of the Lord, create a feeling of reverence, unify us as members, and provide a way for us to offer praises to the Lord. Some of the greatest sermons are preached by the singing of hymns."[5]

Faithful and devoted Christians who were not of our faith created many of our favorite and most inspiring hymns, including "How Great Thou Art," "I Need Thee Every Hour," "I Stand All Amazed," "Because I Have Been Given Much," and "How Firm a Foundation."

In addition to strengthening our church meetings spiritually, sacred hymns can help us control our thoughts, recognizing that our thoughts precede and lead to our actions. Elder Boyd K. Packer taught that we can replace unclean, improper, and degrading thoughts by focusing our attention on sacred music. He suggested that we "choose from among the sacred music of the Church one favorite hymn . . . one with lyrics that are uplifting and the music reverent. Select one that, when it is properly rendered, makes you feel something akin to inspiration.

"Now, go over it in your mind very thoughtfully a few times. Memorize the words and the music. Even though you have had no musical training, even though you do not play an instrument, and even though your voice may leave something to be desired, you can think through a hymn. I suspect you already have a favorite. . . . You can only think of *one*

.thing at a time. Use this hymn as your emergency channel. Use this as the place for your thoughts to go. Anytime you find that . . . shady actors have slipped in from the sideline of your thinking onto the stage of your mind, think through this hymn. . . . Then you will begin to know something about controlling your thoughts." This sacred music "will change the whole mood on the stage of your mind. Because it is clean and uplifting and reverent, the baser thoughts will leave."[6]

We thank the Lord for the pure in heart who have left us their legacy of sacred hymns!

NOTES

1. Conference Report, October 1949, pp. 5–6.
2. Chris Hicks, "Hollywood's Values Clash with Our Own," *Deseret News,* July 19, 1992.
3. Howard W. Hunter, "The Gospel—a Global Faith," *Ensign,* November 1991, pp. 18–19.
4. See Michael Ryan, "Somebody Cares," *Parade,* June 28, 1992, pp. 24–27.
5. *Hymns of The Church of Jesus Christ of Latter-day Saints,* 1985, p. ix.
6. Boyd K. Packer, *That All May Be Edified* (Salt Lake City: Bookcraft, 1982), pp. 38–39.

OUR LORD AND SAVIOR

We live in a day when Lucifer's influence is greater than we ever have known in our lifetime. In terms of the sin, evil, and wickedness upon the earth, we could liken our time to the days of Noah before the flood. No one is immune to affliction and difficulty, whether it be economical, emotional, or spiritual. Immorality, violence, and divorce, with their accompanying sorrows, plague society worldwide.

The only way to find peace, happiness, and security and to overcome the evils of the world and temptations of this generation is through the gospel of Jesus Christ.

Jesus is the head of our church, the Creator of the universe, the Savior and Redeemer of all mankind, and the Judge of the souls of men. Who he is and what he does affected each of us before we were born and will affect us each day of our mortal lives and throughout the eternities. Much of what he is and does is beyond finite human ability to comprehend, but the Holy Ghost has borne witness to my soul of his reality.

I am grateful to know that our Lord and Savior stands at the head of this church and directs it through his servants. This is the Lord's church; it is not a church of men. The brethren of its presiding councils are called of God; their only motive is to serve according to his will in humility "with all [their] heart, might, mind and strength." (D&C 4:2.) The Church bears his name because it is his church. He commanded the Nephites, "Call the church in my name. . . . For if a church be called . . . in the name of a man then it be the church of a man; but if it be called in my name then it is my church, if it so be that they are built upon my gospel." (3 Nephi 27:7–8.) To the Prophet Joseph Smith, the Lord revealed that in the last days, his restored church should be called The Church of Jesus Christ of Latter-day Saints. (See D&C 115:4.)

The Lord told Moses when they spoke together face to face on a high mountain: "Worlds without number have I created; . . . by the Son I created them. . . . But only an account of this earth . . . give I unto you. . . . There are many worlds . . . that now stand, and innumerable are they unto man; but all things are numbered unto me, for they are mine and I know them." (Moses 1:33, 35.)

This brief passage of scripture gives a slight glimpse of the immensity and grandeur of our Lord as Creator. A modern astronomer gives further insight: "The Cosmos is all that is or ever was or ever will be. . . . The size and age of the Cosmos are beyond ordinary human understanding. . . . The dimensions of the Cosmos are so large that . . . familiar units of distance . . . make little sense. Instead, we measure distance with the speed of light. In one second a beam of light travels 186,000 miles. . . . In a year, it crosses . . . about six trillion miles. . . . That unit of length, the distance light goes in a year, is called a light-year. It measures not time but distances—enormous distances. . . . The Cosmos is mostly empty. . . . Worlds are precious. . . . A galaxy is composed of gas and dust and stars—billions upon billions of stars. Every star may be a sun to someone. . . . There are some hundred billion . . . galaxies, each with, on the average,

24

a hundred billion stars. . . . We are hard pressed to find even the cluster in which our Milky Way Galaxy is embedded, much less the Sun or the Earth. . . . The Milky Way contains some 400 billion stars of all sorts moving with a complex and orderly grace. Of all the stars, the inhabitants of Earth know close-up, so far, but one."[1]

In a conversation between God and Moses, God said: "For behold, this is my work and my glory—to bring to pass the immortality and eternal life of man." (Moses 1:39.) God also said: "Mine Only Begotten is and shall be the Savior." (V. 6.)

The immortality and eternal life of man are brought to pass by the atonement of Jesus Christ, our Savior and Redeemer, which is "the most transcendent act that ever has occurred or ever will occur among the children of the Father."[2] It is an act of love for which we should be more grateful than for any other blessing or gift of God. The atonement provides immortality to every person. Immortality is infinite and universal. It provides the opportunity for eternal life, the kind of life that God lives, to those who have faith in Christ, repent of their sins, and obey the laws of the gospel. In a miraculous way, the atonement saves and redeems us from the effects of the fall of Adam, both temporal death at the end of mortality and spiritual death, the separation from our Father.

Only Jesus, because he is the Only Begotten Son, could make the infinite and eternal atonement so we can be at one with our Heavenly Father. When Jesus was born into mortality, his parents were God the Eternal Father (see 1 Nephi 11:21) and Mary, whom Nephi saw in a heavenly vision as "a virgin, most beautiful and fair above all other virgins" (v. 15). He is God's Only Begotten Son, the only one who ever has been or ever will be born on earth of such parentage. Because of his mortal nature, inherited from his mother, he had "the power of mortality, which is the power to die, the power to separate body and spirit."[3] Because of his divine nature, inherited from his Father, he had "the power of immortality, which is the power to live forever; or, having chosen to die, . . . to rise again in immortality."[4]

The Savior said: "I lay down my life, that I might take it again. No man taketh it from me, but I lay it down of myself. I have power to lay it down, and I have power to take it again." (John 10:17–18.)

"It was because this doctrinal reality, this intermixture of the divine and the mortal in one person, that our Lord was able to work out the infinite and eternal atonement. . . . He had power to live or to die, as he chose, and having laid down his life, he had power to take it again, and then, in a way incomprehensible to us, to pass on the effects of that resurrection to all men so that all shall rise from the tomb."[5]

At the time of the Second Coming, Jesus will judge the souls of all mankind in an inevitable judgment. In the gospel of John we read: "The Father judgeth no man, but hath committed all judgment unto the Son: . . . The Father hath . . . given to the Son . . . authority to execute judgment. . . . For the hour is coming, in the which all that are in the graves shall hear his voice, and shall come forth; they that have done good, unto the resurrection of life; and they that have done evil, unto the resurrection of damnation." (John 5:22, 26–29.)

The prophet Mormon wrote: "Ye must all stand before the judgment-seat of Christ, yea, every soul who belongs to the whole human family of Adam; and ye must stand to be judged of your works, whether they be good or evil." (Mormon 3:20.)

Considering all that Jesus is and all he does for us, what should we be doing to show our appreciation? We should go far beyond knowing *about* Jesus and *about* his attributes and mission. We should come to *know* "the only true God, and Jesus Christ, whom [God the Father] hast sent." (John 17:3.) Elder Bruce R. McConkie wrote:

"It is one thing to know about God and another to know him. We know about him when we learn that he is a personal being in whose image man is created; when we learn that the Son is in the express image of his Father's person; when we learn that both the Father and the Son possess certain [specific] attributes and powers. But we know them, in the sense of gaining eternal life, when we enjoy and experience the same things they do. To know God is to think what he thinks, to feel what he feels, to have the power he possesses, to comprehend the truths he understands, and to do what he does. Those who know God become like him, and have his kind of life, which is eternal life."[6]

In other words, to possess a knowledge of Christ, we must become as he is. We become "partakers of the divine nature." (2 Peter 1:4.) He instructed his Nephite disciples: "What manner of men ought ye to be? Verily I say unto you, even as I am." (3 Nephi 27:27.)

One underlying principle runs throughout the Savior's life, mission, and teachings: We are to love one another. He said to his disciples: "A new commandment I give unto you, That ye love one another; as I have loved you, that ye also love one another. By this shall all men know that ye are my disciples, if ye have love one to another." (John 13:34–35.) He said also: "If ye love me, keep my commandments." (John 14:15.)

Imagine for a moment the result if everyone were to love

one another as Jesus loves his disciples. We would have no bickering, quarreling, strife, or contention in our homes. We would not offend or insult one another either verbally or in any other way. We would not have unnecessary litigation over small matters. War would be impossible, especially war waged in the name of religion.

We have numerous testimonies of the reality and divinity of the Lord Jesus Christ. From the time of Adam, the ancient prophets, including the brother of Jared, knew the Savior in his spirit form as Jehovah. During his life on earth, his disciples in Palestine walked and talked with him. They were with him as he taught, when he performed miracles, when he was crucified, and after his resurrection. Peter wrote: "For we have not followed cunningly devised fables, when we made known unto you the power and coming of our Lord Jesus Christ, but were eyewitnesses of his majesty (2 Peter 1:16.)

When the resurrected Lord visited and taught the Nephites, he "stretched forth his hand and spake unto the people, saying: Behold, I am Jesus Christ, whom the prophets testified shall come into the world" (3 Nephi 11:9–10.)

In our day, the Father and the Son visited the Prophet Joseph Smith in the Sacred Grove. Of this visit Joseph wrote: "I saw two Personages, whose brightness and glory defy all description, standing above me in the air. One of them spake unto me, calling me by name and said, pointing to the other—*This is My Beloved Son. Hear Him!*" (Joseph Smith–History 1:17.)

When the Savior accepted the Kirtland Temple as his house, Joseph Smith and Oliver Cowdery "saw the Lord standing upon the breastwork of the pulpit. . . . His eyes were as a flame of fire; the hair of his head was white like the pure snow; his countenance shone above the brightness of the sun; and his voice was as the sound of the rushing of great waters, even the voice of Jehovah, saying: I am the first and the last; I am he who liveth, I am he who was slain; I am your advocate with the Father." (D&C 110:2–4.)

In a heavenly vision, the Prophet and Sidney Rigdon saw and conversed with Jesus Christ and gave this account: "After the many testimonies which have been given of him, this is the testimony, last of all, which we give of him: That he lives! For we saw him, even on the right hand of God; and we heard the voice bearing record that he is the Only Begotten of the Father." (D&C 76:22–23.)

I was fortunate as a young boy attending ward testimony meetings to hear the fervent testimonies of older ward members. Now I counsel those who are more mature spiritually to bear their witness of the truth of the gospel; of the reality of the Savior and his love for each of us; and of the divine calling of his prophets, seers, and revelators. These witnesses will develop testimonies in younger people as did the testimonies of my ward members in me. Parents should bear testimony frequently to strengthen conviction in the hearts of their children.

I am humbly grateful to be one of the "special witnesses of the name of Christ in all the world." (D&C 107:23.) I know that he lives. He is with us, and we can feel his influence in our lives if we are obedient, conform to his teachings, and are prayerful. He wants each of us and the Church to succeed. He also wants members of the Church to carry his teachings to the world, for the Church is the structure through which he can give to the world his message of hope, the hope of salvation, the right to live with our Heavenly Father and his Beloved Son forever.

Notes

1. Carl Sagan, *Cosmos* (New York: Random House, 1980), pp. 4–5, 7, 10.
2. Bruce R. McConkie, *The Millennial Messiah* (Salt Lake City: Deseret Book Co., 1982), p. 15.
3. Bruce R. McConkie, *The Promised Messiah* (Salt Lake City: Deseret Book Co.), 1978, p. 471.
4. Ibid.
5. Ibid.
6. Bruce R. McConkie, *Doctrinal New Testament Commentary,* 3 vols. (Salt Lake City: Bookcraft, 1965–73), 1:762.

How to Build the Spiritual Life

The most interesting drama in all the world is the drama of the human soul and its struggle with good and evil. Literature and the scriptures are filled with interesting accounts of these continuing conflicts, many of which are tragic.

One of the most stirring dramas ever recorded is the one enacted between Jesus and Satan in the wilderness—the story of the Savior overcoming every known temptation that the cunning of Satan, the most evil of the evil, could devise. The drama as portrayed in Matthew lifts the heart, feeds the soul, and inspires courage. It should be read by every Latter-day Saint as a source of strength to withstand temptation.

I call this encounter a drama because, unlike the parables, it was acted out in real life. It was dramatized by Jesus in courageous, heroic deeds. It was not a matter of words alone. The encounter was actual. The principals—two of the most famous in all history—were Jesus, the Son of God in both spirit and flesh, and Satan, God's son of the morning in the world of the unembodied. Satan was a son who had defied his father and, through a violent rebellion, had led astray one-third of all God's children in the premortal existence.

It was inevitable that such a showdown should take place, a battle of the opposing powers, so to speak, a struggle

31

enacted on neutral ground under circumstances that afforded every possible advantage to the aggressor.

Let's follow in detail the events in the life of Jesus that preceded this monumental contest and strengthened him for his ultimate mission. Of his childhood we know little—only that he grew, waxed strong in favor with God and man, and confounded wise men in the temple at the age of twelve.

According to the account in Matthew, on the eve of his final preparation for his life's work, Jesus went from Galilee to the Jordan River to be baptized by John. But John didn't want to perform the ordinance. He said: "I have need to be baptized of thee, and comest thou to me?

"And Jesus answering said unto him, suffer it to be so now: for thus it becometh us to fulfil all righteousness. Then he suffered him. And Jesus, when he was baptized, went up straightway out of the water; and, lo, the heavens were opened unto him, and he saw the Spirit of God descending like a dove, and lighting upon him: and lo a voice from heaven, saying, This is my beloved Son, in whom I am well pleased." (Matthew 3:14–17.)

In other words, John said, "This isn't proper. I am the one who needs to be baptized of you." But Jesus was firm in his request and insisted upon John's proceeding with the baptism, saying, according to one translation, "Come now, this is how we should fulfill all our duty to God. I must do all that's right."

I like that statement. Let us ponder with our hearts and spiritual resources upon this uncompromising statement. If it could become a guide to all our actions, it could transform and renew our lives. No matter how upright we are, it could carry us still closer to the ideal toward which we all are striving. It could transform and improve our families, our neighborhoods, our nation, and even the confused and deteriorating world. If we were each to practice the furthest implications of that statement—"I must do all that's right"—the world would be leavened.

Edward Everett Hale wrote, "I am only one, but still I am one." That is all the world is. It is made up of ones—not populations or mankind, but individuals, persons, you and me, so many "ones." The poet continues: "I cannot do everything, / But still I can do something; / and because I cannot do everything / I will not refuse to do / The something that I can do." That was the undeviating course Jesus took.

But baptism was only a single epic in the preparation of Jesus for his triumph over evil. Immediately afterwards, the heavens were opened and the Spirit of God came down in the form of a dove as the voice of his divine Father was heard, saying, "This is my Beloved Son, in whom I am well pleased." (Matthew 3:17.)

In doing what was right, Jesus was given his Father's wholehearted approval, the highest honor that could come to a worthy son. The word *beloved* and the statement "in whom I am well pleased" highlight the importance of always doing what is right. The objective of each of us should be to live so righteously that we may please Heavenly Father.

Then, the scriptural account records, Jesus was led into the wilderness by the Holy Spirit to finish his preparations for his life's mission. For forty days and forty nights he fasted, but throughout the long ordeal he pondered, prayed earnestly, and gathered miraculous inner strength. Through his example he also tells us how important it is for us to disengage ourselves from the forces and influences that enslave us and hold us prisoners to our physical appetites. Basic to our lives, for example, is the unrelenting demand of our bodies for food and drink. In this experience in the wilderness, Jesus made the instinctive hungers of the flesh subservient to man's eternal nature—his spirit.

When Jesus was weak after his forty-day fast, Satan saw an opportunity to tempt him to gratify his hunger through an unworthy use of his divine powers. Satan, unprincipled and shrewd, suggested that Jesus transform stones into food. The suggestion sheathed a twofold evil: that of demeaning Jesus' divine power for personal gratification, and, in so doing, that of demonstrating that he was indeed the Son of God.

What Jesus said to rebuke Satan constitutes a dependable guide for each of us. He declared without reservation, "Man is not to live by bread alone, but by every word that issues from the mouth of God." To Satan's enticements Jesus gave an emphatic "No!" The reason for this response must be obvious to anyone who has truly pondered life's challenges and purposes. Bread will not and cannot feed people's souls. To accomplish this, obedience to every word of God is what we need. This alone will strengthen the soul and endow it with the power to develop godlike attributes. This is surely wisdom for each of us to consider.

With the rejection by Jesus of his apparently irresistible appeal, Satan did not retreat or concede defeat. Evil is tenacious above all the forces and influences known to man. Satan persisted, and in his second attempt he employed that appeal which, next to the gratification of man's insatiable physical appetites, overwhelms most all other appeals: the appeal to exercise power. The brilliant Lord Acton said, "Power corrupts and absolute power corrupts absolutely." Human beings are prone to dominate. It is a heady intoxicant. They exercise excessive power over their children, their spouses, and their neighbors. They seek power to rule, to command, to dictate.

They seek power to determine the destiny of nations and the utilization of the earth's resources. They crave power to control nearly everything except themselves.

So diabolical is this urge that in a revelation to the Prophet Joseph Smith, God issued a special warning: do not exercise arbitrary and tyrannical power. Heed these eloquent words from the Doctrine and Covenants: "No power or influence can or ought to be maintained by virtue of the priesthood, only by persuasion, by long-suffering, by gentleness and meekness, and by love unfeigned." (D&C 121:41.)

In his desperate effort to conquer the divine nature of Jesus, Satan took him to Jerusalem to the pinnacle of the temple. "Jump off," he commanded, "and prove that you are the Son of God: for the scriptures declare that 'God will give his angels charge of you; they will bear you on their hands, lest you strike your feet against a stone.' It is as simple as that. God will send his angels to keep you from harm."

But Jesus was prepared in the solitude of the wilderness and had made up his mind far in advance of the critical moment when temptation presented its deceitful ploys.

In this regard, there is only one hope for any of us and that is to steel our minds and hearts against temptation, against the enticements of the devil, before temptation arises. This we can best do through pondering in solitude, when we can clearly see, understand, and listen to the promptings of our conscience and the still small voice. This practice is extremely valuable if we are to resist and conquer evil.

Prepared for any temptation, Jesus merely retorted, "You should not tempt the Lord your God." In other words, "Satan, don't you remember—it also says not to put the Lord your God to such a foolish test." I sincerely hope that none of us do this either.

Satan seldom—almost never—gives up; at least he is convinced that his blandishments are futile and that the character and purpose of his intended victim are so invincible that he is wasting his time and effort. But even if Satan does give up for a time, we can never relax our vigilance, for we cannot see the forces of good and evil that surround us from birth. They swirl around us everlastingly.

For Jesus, there was one more assault upon his integrity, one more attempt in the wilderness to discredit him. This time Satan made an appeal to that drive which accomplishes the downfall of the otherwise invulnerable individuals: the almost irresistible hunger to win, to possess, to accumulate money, goods, trinkets, lands, buildings, possessions, wealth. The setting for this enticement was important. As many of us know, when we consider the purchase of a precious stone at some exclusive emporium, we are ushered into an intimate room where the lighting and decor are designed to create a proper atmosphere. The gorgeous jewel is displayed on a piece of velvet, with a spotlight centered on it. Breathlessly and in hushed tones, the sales consultant exults, "Isn't this the loveliest, most exquisite gem you have ever seen?"

So for his third and final attempt to tempt Jesus, Satan next took him to the summit of an exceedingly high mountain and showed him all the nations of the world and all their grandeur and glory. "I'll give it all to you," he glowed, "if you'll only kneel and worship me." This time Jesus dismissed him forthright. "Begone, Satan!" he commanded. "It is written, you must worship the Lord your God, and serve him alone."

This was the climax of the masterful resistance of Jesus to Satan's carefully contrived schemes to lead him astray and rob him of his divine destiny and inheritance.

I tell this story in great detail because of its significance in our lives. I believe that frequent pondering upon its message would decisively strengthen us and give us direction. It would alert us constantly to many of the pitfalls and temptations that are rife today, such as seeking instant gratification, indulging in excessive appetites, falling prey to vanity and pride, and striving for worldly wealth and power. These temptations, made glamorous, are some of the most prevalent evils known to mankind. Being aware of them and pondering the God-given resources that may be utilized to overcome and resist them comprise our safety and salvation.

To muster the faith and the strength essential to cope with his ordeal, Jesus fasted, prayed, and meditated in the wilderness. He withdrew from the multitude to solitude.

Since most people find it relatively easy and convenient to pray, if only mechanically, and to perform in some areas, if only listlessly, I want to emphasize the *pondering* element. I testify that when the quality of the pondering improves, the quality of prayers and performance improves also.

It was in solitude, pondering, and praying that Jesus made ready to battle Satan face to face and resist and overcome all of his enticements. It is not in the hurly-burly of everyday life, amid the pressures of business, society, and even family, that we marshal our greatest strengths, discern our hidden resources, and learn how to utilize our God-given powers in order to fight and vanquish the enemy. It is only in solitude, pondering, and meditating that we live in closest relationship with our Lord. It is also in pondering that we can relive the example of those noble souls of the past who are motivation for us, models of the exemplary life, leaders who have received the revelations and the lofty thought of inspiration.

Our destiny is perfection if we will perform our full duty

as taught by the Church. Jesus set the example by seeking solitude at frequent intervals. It provided priceless opportunities for him to commune with God and angels, to ponder their messages, to identify his strengths and discover how to turn weaknesses into qualities that fortified him for a life of unrivaled beauty and example. It will do the same for us.

The book of Proverbs proclaims, "As [a man] thinketh in his heart, so is he." (Proverbs 23:7.) William James, an illustrious pioneer in psychology at Harvard University, stated, "What commands attention determines action." The process of genuine introspection actuates the heart and determines action. The message is clear and compelling, as further explained by William James in these challenging words: "What the mind attends to continuously, it believes, and what the mind believes it eventually does."

Here again is another strong recommendation for each of us to seek frequent and regular escape to solitude and self-renewal through pondering. According to author Bruce Barton, "It would do the world good if every man in it would compel himself occasionally to be absolutely alone. Most of the world's progress has come out of such loneliness."

President David O. McKay once counseled the General Authorities on the importance of taking the time to ponder and meditate in order to keep spiritually attuned. He said, "It's a great thing to be responsive to the whisperings of the Spirit. We know that when these whisperings come, it is a gift and our privilege to receive them. But they come only when we are relaxed and not under pressure."

In the quiet of our pondering, we can listen to the whisperings of the Spirit. We can listen to the divine voice in such a way as to enhance our faithfulness to the Lord's church and prepare ourselves to withstand temptation.

5

FRUITS OF THE RESTORED GOSPEL

Throughout the ages, the Lord has referred to his people, those who love him and keep his commandments, in words that set them apart. He has called them a "peculiar treasure" (Exodus 19:5), a "special people" (Deuteronomy 7:6), "a royal priesthood, an holy nation" (1 Peter 2:9). Scriptures refer to such people as Saints. As the Savior taught, "by their fruits ye shall know them." (Matthew 7:20.)

In sharp contrast to those who live by gospel principles, I see accounts of people who either ignore or don't understand these principles. Some do not follow gospel standards and live in sin, evil, dishonesty, and crime. The result is untold misery, pain, suffering, and sorrow.

I am reminded of the Savior's teachings when he declared: "Therefore whosoever heareth these sayings of mine, and doeth them, I will liken him unto a wise man, which built his house upon a rock: And the rain descended, and the floods came, and the winds blew, and beat upon that house; and it fell not: for it was founded upon a rock.

"And every one that heareth these sayings of mine, and doeth them not, shall be likened unto a foolish man, which built his house upon the sand: And the rain descended, and the floods came, and the winds blew, and beat upon that house; and it fell: and great was the fall of it." (Matthew 7:24–27.)

This analogy teaches us an important lesson. We cannot have the fruits of the gospel without its roots. Through revelation, the Lord has established those roots: distinctive principles of the fullness of the gospel. They give us direction. The Lord has taught us how we should build our lives on a solid foundation, "a rock," that will withstand the temptations and storms of life.

May I give you some of the major principles of the gospel.

1. *The Godhead.*

One distinctive principle is a true concept of the nature of the Godhead: "We believe in God, the Eternal Father, and in His Son, Jesus Christ, and in the Holy Ghost." (Article of Faith 1:1.) The Godhead consists of three separate, distinct personages who are one in purpose. The Father and the Son have tangible bodies of flesh and bone, while the Holy Ghost is a personage of spirit.

God truly is our Father, the Father of the spirits of all mankind. We are his literal offspring and are formed in his image. We have inherited divine characteristics from him. Knowing our relationship to our Heavenly Father helps us understand the divine nature that is in us and our potential. The doctrine of the fatherhood of God lays a solid foundation for self-esteem. The hymn "I Am a Child of God" states this doctrine in simple terms. Can a person who understands his divine parenthood lack self-esteem? I have known people who have a deep, abiding assurance of this truth and others who understand it only superficially and intellectually. The contrast in their attitudes and the practical effect of these attitudes in their lives is remarkably apparent.

Knowing that Jesus Christ is the Firstborn Son of God in

the spirit and the Only Begotten Son in the flesh gives a far more noble and majestic view of him than if he were just a great teacher or philosopher. He is our Lord, the Redeemer of all mankind, our Mediator with the Father. Because of his love for us, he has atoned for the sins of the world and has provided a way for the faithful to return to the presence of our Heavenly Father.

The dictionary in our LDS edition of the King James Version of the Bible states: "[Jesus] is the greatest Being to be born on this earth—the perfect example. . . . He is Lord of lords, King of kings, the Creator, the Savior, the God of the whole earth. . . . His name . . . is the only name under heaven by which we can be saved. He will come again in power and glory to dwell on the earth, and will stand as Judge of all mankind at the last day."[1]

Jesus stands as the head of The Church of Jesus Christ of Latter-day Saints. We should be everlastingly grateful to him. We should love him with all our hearts and should follow his example.

The Holy Ghost, the third member of the Godhead, is a revelator. He reveals the word of God. He provides the convincing witness that the gospel is true and gives a person a testimony of the divinity of Jesus Christ. He guides us in our choices and in our search for truth.

2. Resurrection.

Next I turn to our assurance of a literal resurrection, the uniting, after mortal death, of the spirit with a body of flesh and bone. Jesus, the first individual on this earth to be resurrected, made the resurrection a certainty for all mankind. This reality is a center point of hope in the gospel of Jesus Christ. (See 1 Corinthians 15:19–22.)

I have seen the contrast between those who have spiritual

41

confidence in the resurrection and others who are confused and uncertain about our postmortal condition. I was inspired by one mother who faced the untimely death of a two-year-old daughter with serenity, despite her deep sorrow. She attributed the peace she felt to her faith in a merciful God and in life everlasting. She was confident that this sweet child was encompassed in the arms of God's love and that she and her daughter would be together again.

3. *Parenting.*

In the Lord's plan, parents are to teach their children during the impressionable and formative years when they develop attitudes and habits that last a lifetime. President Brigham Young wisely recognized that "the time of youth and early manhood is the proper time" to gain mastery over bodily appetites and passions. He warned that "the man who suffers his passions to lead him becomes a slave to them, and such a man will find the work of emancipation an exceedingly difficult one."[2]

We can be so grateful for principles that provide positive, spiritual reinforcement for parental teachings and that direct young people away from the pitfalls Satan has strewn along the path of adolescence and young adulthood.

4. *Word of Wisdom.*

The Word of Wisdom was revealed to the Prophet Joseph Smith in 1833. This revelation has been scrutinized and ignored, attacked and defended, ridiculed and praised. Meanwhile, faithful Saints have observed it as a token of their obedience to God. For many years, they could obey it only on faith, in much the same spirit that Adam offered sacrifice. An angel asked him, "Why dost thou offer sacrifices unto the Lord? And Adam said unto him: I know not, save the Lord commanded me." (Moses 5:6.)

Early members of the Church obeyed the Lord's counsel without the benefit of present medical knowledge, which has validated the physical benefits of their obedience. We now know by scientific evidence what the Saints have known by revelation for more than 150 years.

Imagine the results we would see if people everywhere were to live this law of health and never abuse their bodies with alcoholic beverages, tobacco, and other harmful substances. What magnitude of decline would we see in automobile accidents, illness and premature death, fetal defects, crime, squandered dollars, broken homes, and wasted lives resulting from alcohol and other addictive drugs? How much decrease would we see in lung cancer, heart disease, and other ailments caused by cigarette smoking? Obedience to this commandment brings innumerable blessings.

5. *Welfare principles.*

A sure indicator of true religion is concern for the poor of the earth. This leads us to provide for their needs by acts of charity. James taught, "Pure religion and undefiled before God and the Father is this, To visit the fatherless and widows in their affliction, and to keep [oneself] unspotted from the world." (James 1:27.)

Stated simply, charity means subordinating our interests and needs to those of others, as the Savior has done for all of us. The Apostle Paul wrote that of faith, hope, and charity, "the greatest . . . is charity" (1 Corinthians 13:13), and Moroni wrote, "Except ye have charity ye can in nowise be saved in the kingdom of God" (Moroni 10:21). I believe that selfless service is a distinctive part of the gospel. As President Spencer W. Kimball said, welfare service "is not a program, but the essence of the gospel. *It is the gospel in action.* It is the crowning principle of a Christian life."[3]

43

The Church does substantial but perhaps little-known humanitarian work in many places in the world. Our ability to reach out to others is made possible only to the extent that we are self-reliant. When we are self-reliant, we will use material blessings we receive from God to take care of ourselves and our families and be in a position to help others. Commenting on self-reliance may seem merely to echo the obvious, but this principle runs counter to the trends in today's society that shift responsibility to others. Many Saints have been spared suffering because they have lived by it.

The foundation of self-reliance is hard work. Parents should teach their children that work is the prerequisite to achievement and success in every worthwhile endeavor. Children of legal age should secure productive employment and begin to move away from dependence on parents. None of us should expect others to provide for us anything that we can provide for ourselves.

6. *Missionary work.*

A distinctive part of the Savior's mortal ministry and of the Church in our own day is missionary work. The Savior commanded, "Go ye into all the world, and preach the gospel to every creature." (Mark 16:15.) His disciples, especially Paul, proclaimed the gospel message widely in the years following the Savior's crucifixion. In 1831, the Lord revealed through the Prophet Joseph Smith, "The voice of the Lord is unto all men, and there is none to escape; and there is no eye that shall not see, neither ear that shall not hear, neither heart that shall not be penetrated." (D&C 1:2.)

Today tens of thousands of our missionaries are serving to fulfill the divine mandate to preach the gospel. They bless the people they teach by acquainting them with the fullness of the restored gospel. They bless themselves by the dramatic growth and maturity that come during a mission. Every worthy young man should go on a mission. Worthy young women and couples of the Church can also give invaluable service in the mission field. They all serve as the emissaries of the Lord. We thank them most sincerely.

7. *Chastity.*

Another distinctive characteristic of the gospel is adherence to the Lord's law of chastity. From ancient times to the present, the Lord has commanded his people to obey this law. Such strict morality may seem peculiar or outdated in our day when the media portray pornography and immorality as being normal and fully acceptable. But remember, the Lord has never revoked the law of chastity.

Obedience to the law of chastity would diminish cries for abortion and would go a long way toward controlling sexually transmitted diseases. Total fidelity in marriage would eliminate a major cause of divorce, with its consequent pain and sadness inflicted especially upon innocent children. Honoring vows made in the temple increases the depth of faithfulness between husband and wife.

Of course, members of the Church have their share of faults and weaknesses, but we see abundant evidence that living the gospel does help the Saints to become better. As more people commit themselves to living the gospel with all their heart, might, mind, and strength, they will be examples to their families and friends.

How blessed we are to understand and to have the privilege of living by the sacred, eternal principles of the gospel of Jesus Christ. They are true. They will lead us along the only safe course to happiness, which is "the object and design of our existence."[4]

In conclusion, let me offer this advice and promise. Never

be ashamed of the gospel of Jesus Christ. Partake of the sacrament worthily. Always remember our Lord and Savior. Never defame his sacred name. Do not ridicule the sacredness of the holy priesthood and the ordinances of the gospel.

If you honor this counsel, the spirit of rebellion will never come into your heart. You will be blessed as was Alma, who said: "I have labored without ceasing . . . that I might bring them to taste of the exceeding joy of which I did taste. . . . Yea . . . the Lord doth give me exceedingly great joy in the fruit of my labors; for because of the word which he has imparted unto me, behold, many have been born of God, and have tasted as I have tasted." (Alma 36:24–26.)

In addition, if you will sustain the Lord's anointed, your confidence in them will wax strong. Your family and your posterity will be blessed and strengthened. The abundant fruits of the gospel will enrich your life. Peace and unity will fill your heart and your home.

NOTES

1. LDS edition of the King James Version of the Bible, 1979, Appendix, p. 633, under the heading "Christ."
2. *Letters of Brigham Young to His Sons,* ed. Dean C. Jessee (Salt Lake City: Deseret Book Co., 1974), p. 130.
3. Spencer W. Kimball, "Welfare Services: The Gospel in Action," *Ensign,* November 1977, p. 77. Italics in original.
4. Joseph Smith, *Teachings of the Prophet Joseph Smith,* sel. and arr. by Joseph Fielding Smith (Salt Lake City: Deseret Book Co., 1976), p. 255.

6

DIKES VERSUS LIVING WATER

Much of the Netherlands lies considerably below sea level. Through the process of building dikes to wall out the salty sea, and through pumping the water into canals, the country of the ingenious, resourceful, and doughty Dutch has literally been born of the sea.

The process of wresting the good and precious earth from the bitter ocean waters has been going on for over seven hundred years, and there is no abatement of the struggle in sight. The gigantic dikes, or sea walls, may rise as high as sixty feet above the sea and are often broad enough on the top for a road over which traffic moves. The other side of the dike usually slopes down to green meadows below sea level. Thus, people on the dike can see down the chimneys of the houses nestling below. The fish on the one side are higher than the birds in the trees on the other.

However, there are no dikes tall enough, wide enough, deep enough, or strong enough to give man the security for which his soul cries out, for which he instinctively yearns, and for which he often frantically searches.

In February 1953 news media reported: "A mournful tolling of church bells and the scream of sirens awakened the Netherlanders at 4:00 a.m.; it was already too late. Waves chewed like bulldozers at the historic dikes of Holland, breaking through in at least 70 places, to reclaim what centuries of Dutch ingenuity has taken from the sea. . . . To the north, the flood crest went as high as 30 feet. . . . In a matter of hours, roughly a sixth of the Netherlands' 13,000 square miles—an area where 1,000,000 Dutchmen make their homes—was devastated."[1] The desolation here and in nearby countries had taken a toll of over 1,500 known dead.

When natural disasters strike, we are shocked and saddened at the suddenness and unpredictability of tragedy and the realization that mortal life, at best, is surely a fragile and uncertain spark. The globe is constantly threatened by forces, both man-made and inherent in our dwelling places, so devastating and capricious as to stun and stagger us. And when I speak of forces, I mean the innumerable threats to life of every kind that abound on the earth, in the earth, and around the earth, whether it be here, in the Netherlands, or elsewhere in the broad universe.

Bookstore operators tell us that many of the books on best-seller lists are books on peace and happiness. And since we as a church have the sure answer to mankind's emotional and psychological problems in the gospel of Jesus Christ, it is most urgent that we continue to "lengthen our stride" to reach forlorn, lonely, hungry, and thirsty hearts, and those whose quest is for the truth.

Perhaps I can best emphasize what I feel by recounting the story of a young man named Jack Robertson, who was paralyzed from the waist down as the result of an automobile accident. A teacher at an elementary school in Scottsdale, Arizona, he had developed a burning desire to swim the English Channel and had trained for two long, grueling years, swimming great distances every day under all kinds of weather conditions in order to build up his strength and endurance. He was the first paraplegic ever to attempt the twenty-one-mile swim across the Channel. Because of the strong, treacherous currents, however, a swimmer must cover a far greater distance than that in order to reach the opposite shore.

The day finally came when he was to make his heroic attempt. Wearing a wet suit, flippers, and snorkel, he was carried to the beach at Dover, England, by his cousins, Tom and Don Philabaum, and there he crawled into the sea. Tom and Don accompanied him in a boat and fed him every hour. Jack had hoped to reach the French coast in fifteen hours. "For twelve hours the swim went well," he said. "Then I found myself swimming against the tide." The coast was near, but conditions had decidedly changed. "I gave it all I had," he declared. "Tom was urging me from the boat, saying, 'You've got to do it.' We were so close to France, and yet so far. It was the last few miles that completely drained me. The tides defeated me!" the swimmer exclaimed. His strength ebbed away as he tried to cope with the formidable obstacles in his path.[2]

Life was made for struggle; and exaltation, success, and victory were never meant to be cheap or to come easily. The tides of life often challenge us. To understand why it has to be this way, we should maintain our understanding, our faith, and our courage by a constant rereading of the scripture that tells us, "For it must needs be, that there is an opposition in all things." (2 Nephi 2:11.)

Now may I suggest something that will enable us to maintain our spiritual strength and keep our testimonies vitally alive so that the trails, the storms, and the tides of life will not defeat us. This suggestion is that, above all, we should heed the words of Jesus to the woman at Jacob's well in Samaria

49

when he said, "Whosoever drinketh of the water that I shall give him shall never thirst; but the water that I shall give him shall be in him a well of water springing up into everlasting life." (John 4:14.)

How could one's strength ebb or falter when it may be so dependably and continuously nourished and restored? This scripture tells us clearly that life, at its best and most vigorous, is spiritual and, as such, is the sincere expression of the soul of God. The spiritual self of each of us is that part of us that will never grow old, or become ill, or die, but it must be nurtured and invigorated. Drinking of the living water is the unique recipe, the only way!

NOTES

1. *Time,* February 9, 1953.
2. Recounted from a story published in *Stars and Stripes.*

7

Spiritually Strong Families

During a Manitoba Canada Stake conference a few years ago, Sister Karen Beaumont described her feelings about the raging winter storms that come to their area. She wrote:

"I *love* a winter storm. . . . When the wind starts to blow and the snow begins to fall, a feeling of excitement starts to build. . . . When I can't see the trees at the neighbor's farmyard, . . . I phone my husband! . . . He then picks up the children who are at school. . . . It is hard to describe the feelings I experience as our family is gathered home, and the storm rages outside. . . . And I love it! Everyone is safe; we are together. We have lots of food and water. The longer it lasts, the better. . . . We are shut off from the world. . . . We bask in the warmth of our home and in the warmth of our love. My heart is full, and I am at peace. Sometimes, I wish I could just stay like that forever, with my family gathered around me, protected, shut off from the evil influences of the world. But alas, the storm blows itself out eventually, we dig ourselves out, and off we go to face the world again."[1]

Perhaps all of us at times would like to withdraw and isolate ourselves from the storms of life and from the fiery darts of Satan. However, we must be in the world but not of the world, meaning to go forward in the midst of the sin, evil, and corruption that are in the world but to resist and reject them. Being in the world can be frightening because we live at a time when Satan is becoming more and more bold. The Lord said, "I pray not that thou shouldest take them out of the world, but that thou shouldest keep them from the evil." (John 17:15.)

A recent report titled "Children in Crisis" reflected an aspect of this evil. The editors of a national magazine considered at length what is happening to our children.

"Of the 65 million Americans under 18, [many] live in poverty, 22% live in single-parent homes, and almost 3% live with no parent at all. Violence among the young is . . . rampant. . . . Playground fights that used to end in bloody noses now end in [some fatalities]. Schools that once considered talking in class a capital offense are routinely [checking children] for weapons, questioning them about drugs. . . . A good public education, safe streets, and family dinners—with both father and mother present—seem like quaint memories of a far distant past. . . . The parents of nearly 2,750 children separate or divorce each day. . . . Every day over 500 children ages 10 to 14 begin using illegal drugs, and over 1,000 start drinking alcohol. Nearly half of all middle-schoolers abuse drugs or alcohol or [become involved in immorality]."[2] Data from other nations are equally alarming.

These and many other ills of our society today have their source in the breakdown of the family. If Satan can weaken or destroy the loving relationships among members of families, he can cause more misery and more unhappiness for more people than he could in any other way.

The place to cure most of the ills of society is in the homes, as fortresses of righteousness for protection from the world takes constant labor and diligence. Membership in the Church is no guarantee of a strong, happy family. Often parents feel overwhelmed. Many must accomplish the whole job single-handedly while bearing all of the emotional pain of divorce.

The Lord has provided a plan that will help us to be successful in meeting every challenge that may confront us. In the plan of salvation, *all* families are precious instruments in the Lord's hands to help direct his children toward a celestial destination. The righteous molding of an immortal soul is the highest work we can do, and the home is the place to do it. To accomplish this eternal work, we should make our homes gospel centered. When peace and harmony abound, the Holy Spirit will ever be present. The storms of the evil one can be stopped at the very entrance of our homes.

Let us be sure the spiritual foundation of each home is the rock of our Redeemer, as Helaman taught his sons: "And now, my sons, remember, remember that it is upon the rock of our Redeemer, who is Christ, the Son of God, that ye must build your foundation; that when the devil shall send forth his mighty winds, yea, his shafts in the whirlwind, yea, when all his hail and his mighty storm shall beat upon you, it shall have no power over you to drag you down to the gulf of misery and endless wo, because of the rock upon which ye are built, which is a sure foundation, a foundation whereon if men build they cannot fall." (Helaman 5:12.)

The Lord's standards for building a temple apply also to building spiritual strength in our homes: "Organize yourselves; prepare every needful thing; and establish a house, even a house of prayer, a house of fasting, a house of faith, a house of learning, a house of glory, a house of order, a house of God." (D&C 88:119.) Do we heed this counsel from the Lord? Do we do what he asks? We would do well to build our homes according to this plan, or they are destined to fail.

1. *A house of prayer and fasting:* To make our homes become houses of prayer and fasting, we "pray always, that [we] may come off conqueror; yea, that [we] may . . . escape the hands of the servants of Satan that do uphold his work." (D&C 10:5.) Our families should gather for family prayer morning and night. In addition, we should offer our own individual prayers for our personal needs.

2. *A house of faith:* We can make each home a house of faith by believing in the goodness of God and believing that we *can* live gospel principles and live in peace and security. We need to have the faith to be obedient, to keep trying, and to keep a positive outlook. Sometimes we get discouraged and feel like giving up. But, as an old cowboy once said, "If I get bucked off, I must get back up on the horse and ride on." We can never give up.

When I think of faith, I think of two great Book of Mormon prophets, Nephi and Alma, as models. In faith, Nephi returned to Jerusalem for the plates of brass, "not knowing beforehand the things which [he] should do." (1 Nephi 4:6.) Alma prayed in faith for the repentance of his wayward son, who had become "a very wicked and an idolatrous man" and "was going about to destroy the church of God." (Mosiah 27:8, 10.)

3. *A house of learning and glory:* Every home is a house of learning either for good or otherwise. Family members may learn to be obedient, honest, industrious, self-reliant, and faithful in living the gospel principles, or they may learn something else. Learning the gospel in the homes of Latter-day Saints should be centered on the scriptures and on the words of latter-day prophets.

The Lord has commanded parents to teach their children. King Benjamin instructed parents: "Ye will not suffer your children that they go hungry, or naked; neither will ye suffer that they transgress the laws of God, and fight and quarrel one with another, and serve the devil. . . . But ye will teach them to walk in the ways of truth and soberness; ye will teach them to love one another, and to serve one another." (Mosiah 4:14–15.)

Emphasizing this duty, the Lord cautioned that if parents do not teach their children "to understand the doctrine of repentance, faith in Christ the Son of the living God, and of baptism and the gift of the Holy Ghost by the laying on of the hands, . . . the sin be upon the heads of the parents." (D&C 68:25.)

A personal word of counsel to parents: Teach your children to pray, to rely on the Lord for guidance, and to express appreciation for their blessings. Children learn from you to distinguish between right and wrong. They learn that lying, cheating, stealing, and coveting possessions of others are wrong. Help them to learn to keep the Sabbath day holy and to pay their tithing. Teach them to learn and obey the commandments of God. Teach them that honest labor develops dignity and self-respect. Help them to find pleasure in work and to feel the satisfaction that comes from a job well done.

In 1904, President Joseph F. Smith said to parents: "Do not let your children out to specialists . . . , but teach them by your own precept and example, by your own fireside. Be a specialist yourself in the truth. . . . Not one child in a hundred would go astray, if the home environment, example and training, were in harmony with the truth in the gospel of Christ, as revealed and taught to the Latter-day Saints."[3]

The ideal way to transform your home into a house of learning is to hold family home evening faithfully. The Church has reserved Monday evening for that purpose. In

1915, the First Presidency instructed local leaders and parents to inaugurate a home evening, a time when parents should teach their families the principles of the gospel. The Presidency wrote: "If the Saints obey this counsel, we promise that great blessings will result. Love at home and obedience to parents will increase. Faith will be developed in the hearts of the youth of Israel, and they will gain power to combat the evil influence and temptations which beset them."[4]

President David O. McKay gave the same promise in 1965 and added that the youth will gain power "to choose righteousness and peace, and be assured an eternal place in the family circle of our Father."[5]

In 1976, the First Presidency reaffirmed that "regular participation in family home evening will develop increased personal worth, family unity, love for our fellowmen, and trust in our Father in heaven."[6]

Considering these glorious promises, we would expect every faithful member to be exceedingly diligent in following this prophetic counsel. But, of course, we are all human, and our best plans don't always materialize. Why not? Let it not be for lack of commitment. I know the Lord will keep his promises. I know also that we can keep this commandment if we will organize ourselves and prepare "every needful thing."

I am grateful that my parents and grandparents provided such traditions of learning for our family. My father wrote this account of how his parents taught their children:

"The musical, cheerful voice [of my mother] called, 'Come, children, it is the singing and story hour.' . . . She seated herself in a well-used rocking chair, [and] admonished us to listen carefully, to sing well, and to ask questions. . . . We learned the words of the song by rote, and the meaning or story of each song was made clear to us. 'Joseph Smith's

First Prayer' brought to us the story of the restoration of the gospel and the story of his life was made most impressive. 'Come, Come, Ye Saints' opened the door to the richness of pioneer achievement, faith, and loyalty. . . . A testimony of Joseph Smith's divine calling, of the authenticity of the Book of Mormon, and above all, the reality of our Heavenly Father and his Son, Jesus Christ, were the blessings derived from the family song and story hour."

My father further wrote: "My heart is filled with the gratitude to my angel mother for . . . teaching me the doctrines of repentance, faith, baptism, and the gift of the Holy Ghost. She taught me the power and blessing of prayer, of the actual existence of the Father and the Son, and that Joseph Smith saw and talked to them when a boy fourteen years of age. We knew from her teaching that our Prophet saw other heavenly messengers . . . , and that through them the Church of Jesus Christ was restored to the earth."[7]

When I was a boy, our family home evening took place at the dinner table. It was most pleasant and enjoyable. It was a time when our father would reminisce and tell us about his life. He often told us of his inspirational and exciting experiences while preaching the gospel as a missionary in Germany. Each story seemed to improve the more often it was related. I grew up never doubting that I would become a missionary, and I never lost the zeal that he instilled in my heart. Our mother taught us about the nobility of her pioneer parents and their great faith in the gospel.

Home can literally become a house of glory. Memories of early childhood can become significant in our daily lives.

4. *A house of order:* To instill order in their homes, parents should be in charge, exercise parental authority in righteous dominion, and establish acceptable standards of behavior for

their children, setting limits and adhering to them consistently. By doing so, they will earn the respect of their children, and children will honor their parents, thus unifying families.

Other safeguards of order in our homes include assuring that children are blessed, baptized, and confirmed, and that sons are ordained to the priesthood. In addition, each child should be worthy to enter the holy temple, become a missionary, and receive the crowning blessing of an eternal marriage.

5. *A house of God:* If you will make your home a house of prayer and fasting, faith, learning and glory, and order, it can become a house of God. If you build your home on the foundation rock of our Redeemer and the gospel, it can be a sanctuary where your family can be sheltered from the raging storms of life.

NOTES

1. Unpublished manuscript, Winnipeg Manitoba Stake conference, October 27, 1990.
2. Louis S. Richman, "Struggling to Save Our Kids," *Fortune,* August 10, 1992, pp. 34–35.
3. *Gospel Doctrine: Sermons and Writings of President Joseph F. Smith* (Salt Lake City: Deseret Book Co., 1939), p. 302.
4. James R. Clark, comp., *Messages of the First Presidency of The Church of Jesus Christ of Latter-day Saints,* 6 vols. (Salt Lake City: Bookcraft, 1970), 4:339.
5. *Family Home Evening Manual* (Salt Lake City: The Council of the Twelve Apostles of The Church of Jesus Christ of Latter-day Saints, 1965), p. iii.
6. *Family Home Evening Manual* (Salt Lake City: The Church of Jesus Christ of Latter-day Saints, 1976), p. 3.
7. Joseph L. Wirthlin, *A Heritage of Faith,* comp. Richard B. Wirthlin (Salt Lake City: Deseret Book Co., 1964), pp. 42–43.

8

LITTLE THINGS COUNT

I've been impressed recently with the thought that this life is made up of little things—little things that count a great deal. The Lord has said, "Wherefore, be not weary in well-doing, for ye are laying the foundation of a great work. And out of small things proceedeth that which is great." (D&C 64:33.) I believe that the little things are of great importance in our relationship with ourselves, in our relationships with others, and in our relationship with God.

1. *First, let us consider our relationship with ourselves.*

We must each take proper care to see that the little things regarding our personal life are in order. We must learn to care for our health and our mental well-being. Do we maintain proper exercise to give us the energy and alertness of mind necessary to keep our spirit strong and our attitude positive? Are we wise in our diet? Do we avoid the unnourishing snack that might keep our stomach full but our health quite empty?

Our bodies are truly the result of what we eat and the exercise we receive. If we are not wise, these little things can soon catch up with us to become major health problems that will limit our success and contribution. President Brigham Young once said, "Let us seek to extend the present life to the uttermost, by observing every law of health, and by properly balancing labor, study, rest, and recreation."[1]

The Lord said, "Cease to sleep longer than is needful; retire to thy bed early, that ye may not be weary; arise early, that your bodies and your minds may be invigorated." (D&C 88:124.) Some suffer from too little sleep, and some suffer from too much. This might seem like a little matter, but the wise person learns the value of regular hours and sufficient sleep.

I have often thought that some of the most common little things in our lives are the minutes that pass in each hour of the day. For each human being, time is indeed an indispensable resource. It cannot be ignored or altered. We are compelled to spend it at a fixed rate of sixty minutes every hour. No spigot can be installed to regulate its flow, and no refilling device can replenish its quantity.

The question is not one of managing the clock, but one of managing ourselves with respect to the time we have. As Peter Drucker, the distinguished management consultant, has said, time is "man's most perishable resource," and unless it is managed, nothing else can be managed.[2] Each minute is a little thing and yet, with respect to our personal productivity, to manage the minute is the secret of success.

2. *Second, our relationships with others.*

With regard to our relationships with others, I often marvel at the perfect example the Lord Jesus Christ provides in all aspects of our existence. If we were to meet him, we would find him refreshingly pleasant and perfect in all his relationships and his dealings with each individual. As we study his life and his teachings, especially those found in our modern scriptures, we learn of divine ways to relate to others and grow from our association with our fellowmen.

Do we take the time to remember the simple courtesies that are so important in building relationships with others?

Do we remember the smile, the compliment, the positive note, and the word of encouragement? We should do these things without hesitation. They should be a part of our every-day manner.

Lord Chesterfield said, "Trifles, little attentions, mere nothings, either done or neglected, will make you either liked or disliked in the general run of the world."[3] As an illustration of important little things, consider one of baseball's greats as described in the *Saturday Evening Post:*

> The guy stands 6'4" tall. He weighs 215 pounds. To say he's tough would be an understatement. But he's proved you don't have to drink beer, spit tobacco, laugh at dirty jokes, or curse at the umpires to be a winner in baseball. He's clean as a glass of milk and gentle as a lamb. His name is Dale Murphy.
>
> Chuck Tanner, the manager of the 1986 Atlanta Braves, calls Murphy "Mr. Perfect." In eight seasons with the Braves, the 30-year-old Murphy has compiled team career-batting figures exceeded only by the Hall of Famer Hank Aaron. Tanner and others who have watched, coached, or played with Murphy rhapsodize when asked about the likeable father of four young boys who teaches religion to teenagers in [the] Roswell, Georgia [ward] during the off-season. "God puts somebody down here like Murphy only every 50 years," Tanner says. "I'm not talking just about baseball, either. I'm talking about him as a person. In my opinion, there is no finer fellow on earth."
>
> [And] Willie Stargell . . . praises Murphy. "He just never has a bad word for anybody."[4]

Dale Murphy, along with many others, learned the importance of little things in his relationships with others.

Patience and long-suffering are some of the crowning attributes in dealing with our fellowmen. Whether it be in athletics, in business, or in the Church, if we can acquire these two great attributes, we can work with people and have good influence in their lives.

Elder Richard L. Evans wrote:

> There are battles within ourselves, and battles outside ourselves. The good strives with us . . . and finds itself in competition with the spirit that would tempt us to compromise, to be critical, indifferent, rebellious, to relax our standards, and do what sometime we shall surely regret.
>
> And since everyone has his struggles, his better days and worse ones, his good impulses and less worthy ones, his arguments inside himself; since all of us need understanding, forgiveness, encouragement, all of us would well give compassionate consideration to others. One quality of character most needed in this world is compassion for other people. One of the urgent lessons of life is to learn how to live with imperfect people—including ourselves. And if we are not altogether pleased with us, it should be easy to understand why we are not altogether pleased with others.[5]

Henry Ward Beecher said that "every man should have a good-sized cemetery in which to bury the faults of his friends."

I am reminded of one event when compassion for others played less of a role, and the little matter of listening carefully to the coach's direction made a great deal of difference. I loved to play football in high school and at the University of Utah. I especially remember one game. Our university team faced the University of Colorado in a contest for the conference championship. We were well coached and well prepared.

The star of the Colorado team was Byron White, who was a tremendous athlete, a fast, versatile, and powerful quarterback. His athletic prowess was legendary. His scholastic abilities were equally impressive. He later became a Rhodes scholar and retired recently as an associate justice of the United States Supreme Court.

Our wise coach was Ike Armstrong. His warnings before the game included two simple instructions: do not kick off or punt the ball to White, and never let him get past the line of scrimmage.

We followed his instructions and held Colorado scoreless throughout the first half. Early in the second half, however, White kicked a field goal. We answered with a touchdown and kicked the extra point. We were ahead seven to three at the end of the third quarter.

On the second play of the fourth quarter, we punted. The ball sailed deep into the corner of the field, near Colorado's end zone. White plucked the tumbling ball out of the air at his fifteen-yard line and dropped back to his five-yard line to evade the first of our tacklers. Then with the speed, strength, and agility that had built his reputation, he started upfield and sidestepped every player of the team. I managed only to touch him with my little finger. He ran the entire length of the field for a touchdown—thrilling for Colorado, but disappointing for us.

Later in the fourth quarter, White dashed around his own right and beyond the line of scrimmage and ran fifty-seven yards for another touchdown. The game ended with a score of seventeen to seven. Colorado won the game and the conference championship.

Though we lost, I learned the importance of constant obedience to detail instructions of our leader. Failure to obey our coach's pregame warnings for just two plays—two brief lapses in an otherwise outstanding effort—cost us the game and the conference championship. That is all it took for us to lose something we had worked so hard to achieve.

Other important little things that merit our attention are the small acts of service we perform for our fellowmen. President Spencer W. Kimball said:

> I have learned that it is by serving that we learn how to serve. When we are engaged in the service of our fellowmen, not only do our deeds assist them, but we put our own problems in a fresher perspective. When we concern ourselves more with others, there is less time to be concerned with ourselves. . . .
>
> God does notice us, and he watches over us. But it is usually through another person that he meets our needs. Therefore, it is vital that we serve each other in the kingdom. . . . So often, our acts of service consist of simple encouragement or of giving mundane help with mundane tasks, but what glorious consequences can flow from mundane acts and from small but deliberate deeds![6]

How careful are we in our dealings with our fellowmen? Are we completely honest? No man is worthy of his priesthood calling and no woman is without blame who consciously cheats or deals in dishonest ways.

My father taught me the value of balance in my life. Before my senior year of football and academic pursuits, he encouraged me to go on a mission. He said, "If you don't go now, you'll probably never go." A little over two and a half years later, I found myself newly released from my mission and standing on the streets of Berlin watching the German soldiers board the train to travel to Poland for the Nazi invasion. I was barely able to get home to Salt Lake City because of the immediate eruption of World War II. Had I not followed the advice of my father, I probably would not have had the opportunity to serve a mission.

3. *Third, our relationship with God.*

In fashioning our spiritual bodies, our Heavenly Father took great care to place in each of us every little potential of character, of compassion, of joy, and of knowledge that we would need in our quest for personal growth. The seeds for each godly character trait are in each of us. With that assurance, we are truly able to grow toward godhood as he has commanded us. Remember the Savior's words to the Nephites: "What manner of men ought ye to be? Verily I say unto you, even as I am." (3 Nephi 27:27.)

What if our Creator had neglected some little things—had neglected to place within our spiritual makeup some of the necessary traits to obtain the godly nature we strive for? Suppose he had made some minor mistakes and had overlooked placing within us the ability to be honest, compassionate, or loyal. To us such a matter would seem like an immense disservice. Yet for God it might have been an inconsequential oversight in the creation of so many millions of spirits. But he did not overlook such things. He showed perfect care in the creation of every single spirit, each one unique in specifics but common in potential.

So it must also be in our lives. We must give attention to the detail that will help us grow and develop in our relationship with God. We should heed the words of the prophet Alma to his son Helaman: "But behold I say unto you, that by small and simple things are great things brought to pass." (Alma 37:6.)

President David O. McKay focused our thinking on the purpose of our earthly existence in 1969 when he said: "Keep in mind that man's earthly existence is but a test as to whether he will concentrate his efforts, his mind, his soul upon things which contribute to the comfort and gratification of his physical nature, or whether he will make as his life's purpose the acquisition of spiritual qualities."[7]

The desire to acquire spiritual qualities will lead us to be cautious about the little lies that make us dishonest, or about the small infractions of the Word of Wisdom that turn our bodies and spirits away from what is sacred and worthwhile.

The same desire will cause us to pray a little longer and to be a little more forgiving of our neighbor's faults. We will love more and criticize less. If we seek personal growth in a Christlike direction, we must make as our life's purpose the acquisition of these spiritual qualities.

Certainly one of Satan's prime messages in today's world is that we really do not need to worry about the small matters. Nephi warned us against this attitude when he said:

> And there shall also be many which shall say: Eat, drink, and be merry; nevertheless, fear God—he will justify in committing a little sin; yea, lie a little, take the advantage of one because of his words, dig a pit for thy neighbor; there is no harm in this; and do all these things, for tomorrow we die; and if it so be that we are guilty, God will beat us with a few stripes, and at last we shall be saved in the kingdom of God.
>
> Yea, and there shall be many which shall teach after this manner, false and vain and foolish doctrines, and shall

be puffed up in their hearts, and shall seek deep to hide their counsels from the Lord; and their works shall be in the dark. . . .

For the kingdom of the devil must shake, and they which belong to it must needs be stirred up unto repentance, or the devil will grasp them with his everlasting chains, and they be stirred up to anger, and perish;

For behold, at that day shall he rage in the hearts of the children of men, and stir them up to anger against that which is good. (2 Nephi 28:8–9, 19–20.)

So-called little transgressions are especially serious in our effort to live a life of moral purity. Satan would have us believe that the minor infractions do not need to concern us. Why worry if we do not control our thoughts or if we allow pornographic or immoral entertainment to be part of our lives? Does attending just a few R-rated movies really damage us? Are we so unworthy when we watch just two or three questionable programs on the cable television channels? Are the lewd novels of the day really so bad?

These little rationalizations prompted by Satan will become great detriments to our spiritual growth. Pornography in all its forms—in movies, on television, and in printed form—constitutes a spiritual poison that is addictive and destructive. Every ounce of pornography and immoral entertainment will cause one to lose a pound of spirituality. And it only takes a few ounces of immorality to cause one to lose all of one's spiritual strength, for the Lord's Spirit will not dwell in an unclean temple.

President Ezra Taft Benson gave us excellent counsel: "We counsel you . . . not to pollute your minds with such degrading matter, for the mind through which this filth passes is never the same afterward. Don't see R-rated movies or vulgar videos or participate in any entertainment that is immoral, suggestive, or pornographic. . . . Watch those shows and entertainment that lift the spirit and promote clean thoughts and actions. Read books and magazines that do the same."[8]

Lucifer is a master at step-by-step deception. He can make little things seem harmless when, in reality, they will quickly bind the soul and destroy the spirit. He can make immodest dress and suggestive behavior seem very acceptable. He can cause one to think that a little indiscretion in speech and manner is still quite wholesome. But soon those little steps repeat themselves in an ever-descending pattern until one is at a far-lower level than ever imagined.

I suggest on the positive side that we watch for all possible little opportunities to overcome evil and increase our spiritual strength. We must let virtue garnish our thoughts unceasingly, so that our confidence will wax strong in the presence of God. (See D&C 121:45.)

Remember that prayer is really one of the major factors in our lives. President Ezra Taft Benson related a special experience with prayer:

> Rearing 11 vigorous children to honorable manhood and womanhood on a small farm is no easy accomplishment. Yet, as my father and mother devoted themselves to this task, they never seemed to have any fear of the future. The reason was their faith—their confidence that they could always go to the Lord and He would see them through.
>
> "Remember that whatever you do or wherever you are, you are never alone," was my father's familiar counsel. "Our Heavenly Father is always near. You can reach out and receive His aid through prayer."

Little Things Count

All through my life the counsel to depend on prayer has been prized above any other advice I have ever received. It has become an integral part of me, an anchor, a constant source of strength.

Prayer came to my aid during a most terrifying experience of my early life. I was a missionary in [Sunderland] England. . . . My companion, William Harris, and I were standing back to back, facing a hostile crowd that was swelled by a rowdy element from the pubs, men who were always eager for excitement and not averse to violence.

What had started out to be a customary street meeting soon took on the proportions of an angry, unmanageable mob. Many false malicious rumors had been spread about our church activities.

The crowd started swaying. Someone in the rear called out, "What's the excitement?" Several voices shouted, "It's them bloody Mormons!" This touched off a clamorous demonstration: "Let's get 'em under our feet!" "Throw 'em in the river!"

The mob surged forward and tried to force us to the ground so they might trample us.

In my anxiety, I silently prayed for the Lord's guidance and protection. When it seemed that I could hold out no longer, a husky young stranger pushed through to my side and said in a strong, clear voice: "I believe every word you said tonight. I'm your friend."

As he spoke, a little circle cleared around me. This, to me, was a direct answer to my fervent prayer. The next thing I knew, a sturdy English bobby was convoying us safely through the crowd and back to our lodgings.[9]

Using that great principle of prayer taught by his parents saved the lives of President Benson and his companion.

Consider President McKay's comments regarding the many little things that build our spirituality: "Every noble impulse, every unselfish expression of love, every brave suffering for the right; every surrender of self to something higher than self; every loyalty to an ideal; every unselfish devotion to principle; every helpfulness to humanity; every act of self control; every fine courage of the soul, undefeated by pretence or policy, but by being, doing, and living of good for the very good's sake—that is spirituality."[10]

President McKay also taught us that "spirituality is the consciousness of victory over self, and of communion with the Infinite. Spirituality impels one to conquer difficulties and acquire more and more strength. To feel one's faculties unfolding and truth expanding the soul is one of life's sublimest experiences."[11]

These little things—which, in reality, become such big things—bring perspective to our lives as we learn to conquer them one by one in our effort to gain strength. And this we do in a spirit of humility and gratitude to our Heavenly Father. Alma expressed it best when he said: "And now I would that ye should be humble, and be submissive and gentle; easy to be entreated; full of patience and long-suffering; being temperate in all things; being diligent in keeping the commandments of God at all times; asking for whatsoever things ye stand in need, both spiritual and temporal; always returning thanks unto God for whatsoever things ye do receive." (Alma 7:23.)

President Benson observed in a positive way that all these things are possible. He said, "Our Father's children are essentially good. I think they have, all of them, a spark of divinity in them . . . and they want to do what is right."[12]

This is our religion. We should try to live every day with

70

absolute faith, for we have learned in life that the Lord keeps his promises and watches over those who trust him in spite of their many faults. He has been so good to all of us that we should have a profound conviction that he must really love us in spite of our faults.

I testify to you that so-called little things really do count in the eternal perspective of what it is all about, and that is, to gain eternal life in the presence of our Heavenly Father.

NOTES

1. *Discourses of Brigham Young,* sel. John A. Widtsoe (Salt Lake City: Deseret Book, 1954), p. 186.
2. Peter F. Drucker, *Management* (New York: Harper and Row, 1974), p. 70.
3. *Forty Thousand Quotations,* comp. Charles Noel Douglas (Oyster Bay, New York: Nelson Doubleday, 1917), p. 1822.
4. "Dale Murphy: Baseball's Mr. Nice Guy," *Saturday Evening Post,* October 1986, p. 48.
5. Richard L. Evans, *Thoughts for One Hundred Days,* vol. 4 (Salt Lake City: Publishers Press, 1970), pp. 206–7.
6. Spencer W. Kimball, "Small Acts of Service," *Ensign,* December 1974, pp. 2, 5.
7. David O. McKay, *Conference Report,* October 1969, p. 8.
8. Ezra Taft Benson, "To the Young Women of the Church," *Ensign,* November 1986, p. 84.
9. Frederick W. Babbel, *On Wings of Faith* (Salt Lake City: Bookcraft, 1972), pp. 85–86.
10. David O. McKay, "Something Higher Than Self," *BYU Speeches of the Year,* October 12, 1965, pp. 4–5.
11. David O. McKay, *Conference Report,* April 1949, p. 17.
12. Ezra Taft Benson, Regional Representatives' Seminar, October 4, 1973.

POWER TO CHOOSE

The Lord has placed us here on this earth to learn from our experiences, both good and bad, and to prove whether or not we will be obedient. One of the most important gifts he gave us before our sojourn in mortality is the power to choose, the power within us to control our own ultimate destiny. So important was this gift that we, as premortal beings, fought in a war in heaven to preserve it. God cast Satan and one-third of the hosts of heaven out of his presence because they opposed this principle of agency. Our choice to follow the Savior and accept the principle allowed us to come to this mortal probation.

The choices we make from now and through the balance of our mortal existence will determine the degree of glory we will attain in the hour of final judgment or the final graduation ceremony. President Ezra Taft Benson told a graduating class several years ago:

"I believe that our Heavenly Father expects all members of his church to become exalted in the celestial kingdom. We are not striving for the lower kingdoms. We are not candidates for the telestial or terrestrial kingdoms. But we are candidates for the celestial kingdom and the highest glory in that kingdom. . . . Exaltation requires a great deal. . . . This means not just going to church, but living the gospel in your homes;

not just holding the priesthood, but magnifying it as you live a life of happiness and joy. This is not happiness as measured by the world."[1]

A good beginning can lead to a good ending. Therefore, the choices we make now are among the most important of any we will make in the scheme of life. If we have not been spiritually inclined, now is the time to become totally committed. If we have not married, now is the time to be serious about finding a mate. If we have not been paying our tithing, now is the time to begin obeying the law of the tithe consistently. Life to this point has been a time of deep preparation.

Even if we have wasted opportunities and even if we have made some truly regrettable mistakes, we can start today to make amends to do and be what is right.

Exercising our God-given power to choose, we can:

> *Choose to love . . . rather than hate.*
> *Choose to laugh . . . rather than cry.*
> *Choose to create . . . rather than destroy.*
> *Choose to persevere . . . rather than quit.*
> *Choose to praise . . . rather than gossip.*
> *Choose to heal . . . rather than wound.*
> *Choose to give . . . rather than steal.*
> *Choose to act . . . rather than procrastinate.*
> *Choose to pray . . . rather than curse.*
> *Choose to live . . . rather than die.*[2]

I believe that the best choices in life can be condensed into one sentence: Always choose the light rather than darkness. In doing so, I suggest four choices we can make that will keep us in the light:

1. *Choose the light of the Lord.*

The Lord is the truth and the light. If we choose to know

him, then we will walk in the light. Jesus said, "I am the light of the world: he that followeth me shall not walk in darkness, but shall have the light of life." (John 8:12.)

We can choose to know the Lord by reading the scriptures every day; by communicating with him in fervent prayer at least morning and night, and in times of trial, every hour or more, if needed; and by keeping his commandments. Remember, "Hereby we do know that we know him, if we keep his commandments. He that saith, I know him, and keepeth not his commandments, is a liar, and the truth is not in him. But whoso keepeth his word, in him verily is the love of God perfected: hereby know we that we are in him." (1 John 2:3–5.)

2. *Choose to seek knowledge, which is truth and light.*

A revelation given to the Prophet Joseph Smith states: "The glory of God is intelligence, or, in other words, light and truth." (D&C 93:36.)

I remember that my mother was always reading and studying. She felt the importance of renewing her mind. She tried to improve herself a little every day. She worked hard to perfect her lessons for the Mia Maids, Laurels, and Relief Society members. She continued to read and study throughout her long life.

3. *Choose the light of love in your life.*

Where there is love and it is expressed, the Spirit is present. The Savior taught: "A new commandment I give unto you, That ye love one another; as I have loved you, that ye also love one another. By this shall all men know that ye are my disciples, if ye have love one to another." (John 13:34–35.)

"He that saith he is in the light, and hateth his brother, is in darkness even until now. He that loveth his brother abideth in the light, and there is none occasion of stumbling in him. But he that hateth his brother is in darkness, and walketh in darkness, and knoweth not whither he goeth, because that darkness hath blinded his eyes." (1 John 2:9–11.)

"Whosoever doeth not righteousness is not of God, neither he that loveth not his brother." (1 John 3:10.)

"He that loveth not knoweth not God; for God is love." (1 John 4:8.)

4. *Choose to live by the light of the Spirit.*

By choosing the light of the Lord, knowledge and truth, and the light of love in our lives, we will be qualified to live by the light of the Spirit. If we cultivate a heart that is constantly in tune with the Spirit of the Lord, our lives will be enriched. We will be able to make good decisions, and we will be comforted in times of trial and adversity.

We could compare learning to live by the Spirit with the way a pianist prepares for a concert. A pianist cannot cram his knowledge of music and his playing skill into one week or even one month of solid practice to prepare for a concert. But he prepares himself through consistent, diligent practice, day by day over a long period of time. Our spiritual preparation requires the same kind of effort, "line upon line, precept upon precept, here a little and there a little." (2 Nephi 28:30.)

As we choose to live by the light of the Spirit, the greatest example on how to prepare ourselves spiritually is the pattern set forth by our Lord and Savior Jesus Christ.

Notes

1. Ezra Taft Benson, Greeting, Brigham Young University commencement, April 18, 1986.
2. Og Mandino, *Three Volumes in One: The Greatest Miracle in the World* (New York: Bonanza Books, 1985), pp. 412–13.

10

SHARING OUR LIGHT

As Latter-day Saints, we know that whatsoever is truth is light. (See D&C 84:45.) The source of this light is our Lord and Savior, Jesus Christ, who is "the light, and the life, and the truth of the world." (Ether 4:12.) In possessing this light, we can shine among our fellowmen through our lives and deeds, influencing them also to glorify our Father in Heaven.

Jesus wants us to know him because of the transforming power of that knowledge and because of the indescribable joy it brings into our lives. But the influence of the gospel is to extend beyond each individual. It is to be as a light that dispels the darkness from the lives of those around us. None of us are saved solely and simply for ourselves alone, just as no lamp is lighted merely for its own benefit.

The responsibility that no person can escape is that of wielding a personal influence. Daily words and actions influence the entire world. We each carry an atmosphere that radiates from us and that in some manner or degree affects others. We cannot escape it. We must so live our lives that we set the proper example to those about us. We are each a light, and it is our duty not to have that light hidden under a bushel, but to set it upon a hill, that all persons may be guided by it. The Lord has commanded us in these latter days:

"Arise and shine forth, that thy light may be a standard for the nations." (D&C 115:5.)

This divine counsel is given to us in the holy scriptures; Jesus addressed his disciples, saying: "Ye are the light of the world. A city that is set on an hill cannot be hid. Neither do men light a candle, and put it under a bushel, but on a candlestick; and it giveth light unto all that are in the house. Let your light so shine before men, that they may see your good works, and glorify your Father which is in heaven." (Matthew 5:14–16.)

In these challenging times, we must take advantage of every opportunity to let our light shine in a world that is groping in spiritual darkness.

Those of my generation remember some of the necessary blackouts imposed during the second World War. To remain undetected by enemy bombers overhead or to conceal their location from the enemy, entire cities would be blacked out. Windows would be covered, shades drawn, lights snuffed out. Troops were told that in complete darkness, the flickering of a single match could be seen for more than a mile. In battle, the infantryman was cautious about showing light in any form lest he reveal his position.

Under these trying circumstances, people dreamed of freedom and normalcy and for better times to come. They talked about it. They wrote songs about it. I remember the haunting strains of the song "When the Lights Go On Again All Over the World." The war finally ended and lights did go on again, all over the world, and people rejoiced.

In many ways, however, our cities today are still blacked out. Electric lights may glimmer in many colors and with great intensity, but the spiritual candles of many are dim.

Light is needed as never before in a world enveloped in spiritual darkness.

Many exciting challenges lie ahead for us, both young and old. Serious problems need to be solved. The threat of war is ever-present. Personal freedoms are being eroded constantly by too much government. We need to combat the increasing dependence upon government or other agencies to provide for us those things that we ought to provide for ourselves. The burden of physical, as well as spiritual, pollution and erosion is increasing. Personal and national debts are beyond control. We have challenges of taking the gospel to millions of people in nations throughout the world.

How can we, a relatively few, bring light to a world groping in spiritual darkness? Many would consider it an over-simplification to say that living the gospel of Jesus Christ gives answers to all the world's problems. As simplistic as this may sound, however, it is true. Of this I testify.

In reading the Book of Mormon, I have always been especially interested to learn of a time when conditions were similar to our own conditions today. Alma the Younger served as the political leader or chief judge, as well as the presiding high priest in the Church. He delivered up the judgment seat in favor of missionary work and confined himself wholly to the testimony of the word. He challenged his associates to be spiritually born of God, asking "Have ye experienced this mighty change in your hearts?" (Alma 5:14.)

Alma realized that he would have a greater influence upon his people and his nation through turning their hearts to God than he would with all of the political power men could bestow. This was true in the time of Alma. It is just as true today.

Thus, the cumulative radiance of our candles, as members

of The Church of Jesus Christ of Latter-day Saints, can illuminate a world filled with darkness, leading many others into the glorious light of the gospel. Darkness, after all, is the absence of light.

As our lights glow and illuminate, we must be certain that we are walking in the straight and narrow way prescribed by the Savior. If we fail in this mandate, we might be compared to a lighthouse built in a deceptive location, luring trusting sailors to their watery deaths. We must be certain that our lights are leading in the right direction. We might well ask ourselves, "What will happen in my family, in my community, in my church, if people follow my light?" Or we might ask, "What kind of a world would this world be if everyone were just like me?"

If we are to be a light to the world, we must guard against letting our light flicker or go out. Elder Neal A. Maxwell expressed the thought in this way:

"Just as the unsheltered flame flutters when brushed by gusts of wind, and just as the unsheltered flame flickers and sputters when dashed by rain, so our own lights can be threatened; and we as individuals need to avoid deliberately those conditions which dampen our light. We also need to search out and to create those conditions in which our light can burn more brightly and steadily. We need an appropriate blend of challenge and refuge, and of search and sanctuary— we need to create and to preserve the proper conditions for burning."[1]

If we are to guard against those conditions that dampen our light, it might be well to consider some basic principles and areas we must be aware of.

First, integrity. The standard by which we should measure our integrity is not the world's standard but the standard the

Lord has given us. Integrity is many things. It is giving an honest day's work to our employer. Integrity is honesty in what we say or imply, avoiding such business practices as misrepresenting ourselves or our products. Integrity implies faithfulness in marriage and family relationships. It means being loyal and true with each other and, most importantly, with ourselves and our Heavenly Father. I know of no way to make our lights shine brighter than by having complete integrity at all times with everyone.

Second, obedience. Nothing will smother the flame of the spirit more quickly and completely than disobedience or transgression. Obedience, therefore, assumes a central role in keeping our lights shining. It includes a clear understanding and frequent application of the principle of repentance for the times we may falter.

We have many good examples established by our associates and leaders. I think, for example, of President Marion G. Romney, a valiant leader and friend. How brightly his candle burned! When President Spencer W. Kimball counseled members to plant gardens, President Romney immediately tore up a section of his lawn and enlarged his garden space. He wanted to be one of the first to obey. May I share with you another example of his integrity and devotion in an example from his life that he related:

> When I was set apart for my mission, . . . Brother Melvin J. Ballard laid his hands upon my head and said, among other things, "One never gives a crust to the Lord without receiving a loaf in return."
>
> A few years ago, I had just finished paying for my home. For the first time in my life I was getting to the place where I could afford to buy my wife an ice cream sundae without feeling we would have to go without

some necessity. Then, as I sat in general conference one Saturday morning, I unexpectedly heard my name read off as one of the General Authorities of the Church. Shortly thereafter I learned that my income would be cut in two—that is, I would receive a living allowance which was just about half of what I was then making practicing law.

Our ward was then about to begin building a meetinghouse. The bishop came to me and said, "Brother Romney, we think you ought to pay X dollars." . . . I looked at the bishop, and I felt I couldn't say what I felt, but I said, "Well, I'll pay it, but I'll have to pay it in installments because I don't have the money and I don't think I have the credit to borrow it." So I paid and paid, until finally I had only two payments left. I never had felt quite right about the bishop's judgment.

Then one day I read in the Book of Mormon the statement that "He that giveth the gift and not with real intent, it is accounted unto him the same as if he had retained the gift." (This isn't the exact quotation, but it is the exact thought.) I realized then that I was out about a thousand dollars. I remember that after I had paid the last installments, I paid a few more to try to convince the Lord that I had paid with real intent. Later, the bishop came to me and said, "Brother Romney, we didn't get enough money on that first assessment, so we think you should pay X dollars more." I didn't hesitate again; I didn't want to have to make any extra payments to show the Lord I had done it with real intent.

Well, about that time the stake president came to tell us they were building a stake house and needed a contribution—so we paid it. And then, the week we got it paid off, the stake was divided, and the stake house went into another stake. Then they started to build another stake house in our present stake, to which we have had the pleasure of making contributions. The making of contributions has never hurt us.

I am sure that everyone who makes a contribution to the building of these meetinghouses—or toward the financing of any other thing in the kingdom of God—is blessed. He receives far more than he could purchased with the money had he kept it. So I don't feel sorry for you people who have made the greatest contribution. I envy you. You will all receive blessings according to your contributions. No man can give himself poor in building the kingdom of God.[2]

Countless souls were lifted through the shining light of President Romney. Each of us can be a light for others in much the same way, quietly living exemplary lives.

As members of The Church of Jesus Christ of Latter-day Saints, we can take strength from one another, lifting and helping along the way. To illustrate this point, let me share an experience a friend of mine related to me.

He said that as a priesthood leader, he had assigned one of his faithful members, whom I'll call Bill, to fellowship and encourage David, a fellow quorum member, into activity in the Church. The bishop and Bill worked together, uniting in love and concern as they fasted and prayed in behalf of David. They visited frequently with his family, taking an interest in their affairs and helping them through a rather traumatic crisis. In many actions and expressions, they let him know of their love and persuaded him that he was wanted and needed.

Cautious at first, David began tentatively to participate in church activities, and soon he warmed to the fellowshipping of the Saints and began to feel an increased outpouring of the Spirit.

Time passed. In the meantime, Bill faced some serious problems of his own. His faith was tested. Through a series of setbacks his candle grew dim; his light flickered and went out. The same concerned priesthood leader noted the turn of events. This time it was David who was sent to rescue the very one who had once rescued him and helped rekindle his flame.

Yes, there is great safety in being our brother's keeper, for he is our keeper too. In his poem "A Creed," Edwin Markham expressed it this way:

> *There is a destiny that makes us brothers;*
> *No one goes his way alone:*
> *All that we send into the lives of others*
> *Comes back into our own.*

To be a light for others, we ourselves must live in the light. To do this, we must make correct choices, walking in the ways of the Lord.

There are places where our lights shine the brightest. Elder Theodore M. Burton of the Seventy shared this experience with us:

When I was a young boy, I went with my father to inspect a mine in Nevada. We each had flashlights, but took no extra batteries with us, for we did not expect to be in the mine very long. But the tunnel was longer, colder, and deeper than we anticipated. Before we got to the end of the mine, where the mineral was, father told me to turn off my flashlight to save my batteries. By the time father had finished inspecting the mine, his flashlight began to dim, and he suggested we had better turn

83

back. Before long his flashlight gave out completely, and I can still remember—until I again turned on my light—the panic I felt to be in such cold and utter blackness. Although my own batteries gave out before we reached the mine entrance, we were by then guided by the dim light coming from the mouth of the tunnel. How good it felt to see the light increase coming from the mouth of the tunnel. How good it felt to see the light increase as we made our way back to the entrance and found ourselves in warm, brilliant sunlight.

I have since wondered how anyone could knowingly prefer to live where it is dark and cold. How could anybody willingly prefer darkness and misery over light and warmth? Yet darkness, cold, and misery will be the lot of those who willingly and knowingly reject the Lord. John wrote, "God is light, and in him is no darkness at all." (1 John 1:5.)[3]

I remember passing a dark and dirty pool hall in years past. When it changed ownership, the new owner spared no expense to clean up the place. He put bright lights where dim ones had been. He painted with clean new colors over dark and dingy walls. He replaced painted windows with clear glass that invited in the sunshine. The "new place" smelled clean and fresh and was bright, shining, and inviting. But what happened next was an interesting phenomenon. Most of the old customers stayed away; they chose darkness rather than light. A decrease in business was followed by a period of planned neglect. Clear windows become smoke-filmed and fly-specked. Bright lights were turned out. Walls became dirty. Eventually the old customers returned to their comfort zone in the darkness.

Familiarity with darkness can eventually erode our sensitivity until we choose darkness rather than light. Let us seek the light and keep our own lights shining, thus inviting the Spirit of the Lord into our lives, our homes, and the lives of our children and neighbors.

NOTES

1. "On Being a Light," address given at the Salt Lake Institute of Religion, January 2, 1974.
2. Notes from an address given by President Romney at the dedication of the Butler Second Ward building, Salt Lake City, November 12, 1961.
3. Theodore M. Burton, "Light and Truth," *Ensign,* May 1981, p. 28.

11

Restoring the Lost Sheep

A young man sought out a wise man who was recognized far and near for his good judgment. He asked for his expert advice on how to attain new heights of achievement in his field of endeavor.

"Come with me," said the wise man. Taking the youth to a nearby stream, he immersed him and held him under the water. When the young man was released, he was nearly drowned and came up fighting for breath, gasping, "Air, air, give me air!"

"There," said the wise man, "that's the first lesson. When you want to succeed as badly as you wanted air, you will attain your goal. You will succeed."

Desire, burning desire, is basic to achieving anything beyond the ordinary.

Why do I begin with this story? Because desire in everyone involved is the first step in helping less-active Saints to become fully active. Those who are successful love what they are doing. It is a well-known fact that our attitude must be right before we can *do* what is right.

Elder Dean L. Larsen of the Seventy summarized this idea in these words: "When we understand what is right and what is wrong, we are in a position to exercise our freedom in making choices. In so doing, we must stand accountable for our decisions, and we cannot escape the inevitable consequences of these choices. Such freedom to exercise moral agency is essential in an environment where people have the highest prospects for progress and development."[1]

Jesus concerned himself primarily with the teaching of fundamental principles, and these principles had to do with the spiritual and mental condition of the individual. The Savior knew that if one's mental state is right, most everything else would be right. But if the mental state is wrong, little can be accomplished in a person's life.

It is no wonder, then, that Nephi admonished his people to "feast upon the words of Christ; for behold, the words of Christ will tell you all things what ye should do." (2 Nephi 32:3.)

Jesus said, "Not every one that saith unto me, Lord, Lord, shall enter into the kingdom of heaven; but he that doeth the will of my Father which is in heaven." (Matthew 7:21.) "Enter ye in at the strait gate." (Matthew 7:13.)

President Marion G. Romney expressed most clearly what is meant: "It is not enough to do our best. Unless we do all we can, we do less than we ought. We must succeed in doing what is necessary. Unless we get the job done, it is not enough."

In seeking to strengthen those who are less active, we are concerned with four general groups:

1. Lifetime members who have never been active and, as a result, ofttimes raise their families in inactivity.

2. New converts who become spiritually disaffected and fall away, usually in their first few years of membership.

3. Active members who slip into transgression or have other problems that cause them to fall away. Often their problems include lack of knowledge and testimony of the

87

gospel, hurt feelings that result in attitudes of unworthiness and guilt, and sometimes fear of participation in church assignments.

4. Youths who are caught up in the philosophies or behavior of the world and stray from their church commitments. Some of these youths are persuaded by worldly attitudes of instant pleasure. Some are influenced by peer groups that take nothing seriously until the realities of life force them to.

This work of reclaiming the lost sheep, as Jesus so vividly expressed it, must receive top priority by every stake, ward, branch, quorum, and auxiliary leader. All less-active members should be considered candidates for activation regardless of their response to any previous approach. We must use kindness, patience, long-suffering, love, faith, and diligence. They must feel our genuine concern and untiring love.

For individuals to become fully active in the Church, they generally must experience a spiritual conversion and a social integration. We should strive to teach them the gospel and to extend warmth, genuine friendship, and fellowship to them.

At a stake conference I heard a story of member activation that moved me deeply. The bishop of one of the wards in the stake took a keen interest in arousing less-active brethren to church activity. He knew that the first step was one of communication, and that he must have a meaningful visit with each less-active brother, so he began by telephoning one of them.

The wife answered the phone and said, "Bishop, I surely appreciate your call. My husband is outside, but I will have him come to the phone."

When the husband heard that it was the bishop who wished to speak to him, he attempted to sidestep the phone call and responded, "Tell the bishop that I'm out sawing logs," adding, with a humorous touch, "Tell him I'm dead."

The brother spoke the truth more literally than he realized. It was true. He was sawing logs, and, tragically, he was dead to the spiritual things of his life.

A good wife, however, is a mighty force in any man's life, and, in a kindly manner, this woman persuaded her husband to come to the phone.

Then the bishop, using the power of suggestion and in a friendly voice, said, "I should very much appreciate having a visit with you for a few moments this evening in my office." The brother couldn't refuse such a warmhearted invitation, and a meeting took place.

The testimony of the bishop and his deep concern kindled a fire in the heart of the less-active brother, and he agreed to join the temple preparation class that was about to begin.

Each session, taught by a tactful teacher with a great knowledge of the truth and an inspiring testimony, motivated the less-active brother. He resolved to strengthen his family and bind them together eternally through the blessings of the temple.

This good brother may still be sawing logs, but there is now much more. He has added for himself an indescribable dimension of happiness, as well as joy to the lives of each and every family member.

In another ward, the bishop assigned his two most effective home teachers to work with one particular family. The husband and father had not attended church for many years, even though he held the office of elder in the Melchizedek Priesthood. The bishop approached the couple and asked if the specially selected home teachers could come and teach them the gospel in weekly visits to their home. The family agreed, and the teachers proceeded to bring gospel lessons tailored to the needs and desires of the family.

The bishop also helped by interviewing the couple every few weeks. The husband usually went golfing on Sundays and had no desire to change his lifestyle at first. During one interview, the bishop said to him, "You've got to get going on spiritual matters so that you won't lose your fine family." This caused the brother to think deeply about important issues, and within a couple of weeks he asked for another interview with the bishop and said that he had started paying tithing and that he and his wife wanted to set a goal of being sealed in the temple.

As this family became active, their whole attitude changed, and they seemed to be very happy to embrace the gospel principles and make the necessary changes in lifestyle.

In the case of yet another less-active family—parents and their five children—the home teachers lived in the same neighborhood. They first showed genuine friendship and neighborly concern until they felt they could talk with the family in a serious manner. They made an appointment, and as they met with the family, they asked if they could begin teaching them the gospel in weekly sessions in their home. They assured the family members that they would not pressure them in any way and that their visits would be designed to teach the doctrines of the Savior and answer questions they might have. Within a few weeks, the home teachers took the family to church, and soon the family began to attend on their own. The bishop interviewed the couple and helped them to set goals for the husband to be ordained to the Melchizedek Priesthood and for them all to be sealed in the temple.

The bishop reports that it was touching to see this family

all sealed for time and eternity. The sealing room in the temple was filled with friends and members of the ward.

The reactivated family members now bear strong testimony to the truth of the gospel, and many in the ward say they have never seen people change so much.

The president of an elders quorum in a stake in Brazil reported phenomenal success in reactivating fifteen elders in his quorum. I asked, "How did you accomplish this?" He said, "The quorum presidency and the home teachers visited them often. They knew that we really cared for them." The testimonies of the fifteen elders were strengthened, and they and their families are now active in the Church.

The Lord has said in modern revelation, "If it so be that you should labor all your days in crying repentance unto this people, and bring, save it be one soul unto me, how great shall be your joy with him in the kingdom of my Father!" (D&C 18:15.)

I wish I could engrave on every heart what I so keenly know and feel. I bear unwavering testimony that our Heavenly Father and His Divine Son, Jesus Christ, rule and reign, and that we must all understand that the gospel is everlasting. It is forever and applicable to all, and each of us is to be held accountable. May the Lord bless us in this important work.

NOTE

1. Dean L. Larsen, "Self-Accountability and Human Progress," *Ensign*, May 1980, p. 76.

12

Let Us Learn Our Duty

Inscribed beneath Robert E. Lee's bust in the Hall of Fame are his words: "Duty is the sublimest word in our language. Do your duty in all things. You cannot do more. You should never wish to do less."

Most of us don't mind doing what we *ought* to do when it doesn't interfere with what we *want* to do, but it takes discipline and maturity to do what we ought to do whether we want to or not. Duty is too often what one expects from others and not what one does. What people think and believe and plan are all very important, but what they *do* is the thing that counts most. It is a call to throw out selfishness and to think of the common good of all.

The Prophet Joseph Smith was told in an impressive revelation: "Wherefore, now let every man learn his duty, and to act in the office in which he is appointed, in all diligence. He that is slothful shall not be counted worthy to stand, and he that learns not his duty and shows himself not approved shall not be counted worthy to stand." (D&C 107:99–100.)

We must always remember that duty reminds us we are stewards of all that our Creator has entrusted to us. When we accept duties willingly and faithfully, we find happiness. Those who make happiness the chief objective of life are bound to fail, for happiness is a by-product rather than an end in itself. Happiness comes from doing one's duty and knowing that his life is in harmony with God and his commandments.

Doing our duty is the best way to solve our problems. The proper pattern of duty has been set by those who have gone before us and is continued today by devoted teachers and leaders throughout the Church.

Every successful man and woman in the history of the world has known his or her duty and has had a firm desire to fulfill it. The Savior has a perfect sense of duty. Even though what was required of him surpassed the limits of human capabilities, he submitted himself to his Father's will and fulfilled his divine duty by atoning for the sins of mankind.

Joseph Smith was true to his calling and fulfilled his duty even in the face of severe persecution and great personal sacrifice. He persevered, he endured, and he accomplished the restoration of the true gospel of Jesus Christ.

Brigham Young also carried out his responsibilities. Over a period of many years of faithful service and duty, he brought the Saints to the valley of freedom and established a great and mighty empire. He was duty-bound and thereby achieved great things.

President Spencer W. Kimball accepted the charge to take the gospel to the ends of the earth. He faithfully pursued his duty and was a wonderful example to us in all that he did to spread the gospel of love. The result is a worldwide Church and the fulfillment of latter-day prophecy.

These great men all had the agency to choose. They might have chosen to follow a path easier than the one where duty led. But they did not. Certainly their duty did not always lead to personal comfort or casual convenience. Their duty frequently meant great sacrifice and personal hardship. Nevertheless, duty they chose, and duty they performed.

Life requires us to perform many duties—some routine, others more meaningful and important. An integral part of duty is to set the proper example and to take every opportunity to bolster others along this uphill road of life. This might be done with an encouraging word, a compliment, a handshake—any indication of caring. And we need to keep in mind that as we learn our duties well here, we also are preparing for the performance of eternal duties.

Every member of the Church—every man, woman, and child—is faced with an obligation to fulfill his duty. Every member of the Church is commanded to live the laws of God and keep his commandments. Each has the duty to pray daily, study the scriptures, draw close to the Savior, and serve others. Each should partake of the sacrament worthily and labor to strengthen the influence of the Holy Ghost in his or her life.

Each father has the duty to provide for his family and to teach them by example to obey the statutes of God. Each woman has a glorious duty to bring children into this life and to create a loving, learning, and supporting home atmosphere. Together, parents have the divine duty to bring up their children in the "nurture and admonition of the Lord." (Ephesians 6:4.)

It is the duty of children to obey their parents, to learn, and to help with household chores. They carry the scriptural charge not to contend and quarrel with one another but to accept their part in fostering family unity and progress.

All have the duty to share the gospel with others and to serve formally and informally as missionaries. All have a duty to identify their deceased ancestors and to help bring to them the blessings of the temple. All should diligently strive to be temporally prepared and to care for the poor and the needy. All should seek to strengthen those who are less active in the Church and to magnify their callings in their wards and stakes by giving faithful and devoted service.

These are some of our duties. They may not always be exciting or even enjoyable, but they are important. They will refine the spirit and strengthen the soul. They will aid the work of the Lord in great measure.

The Lord has told us, "Be not weary in well-doing." (D&C 64:33.) Being true to one's duty is the mark of a true disciple of the Lord and a child of God. May we be valiant in our duty, stay in step, and not fail in our most important task: keeping our second estate. Being true to our duty will bring us to God.

13

HE WILL BE IN OUR MIDST

In January 1831 the Lord, through the Prophet Joseph Smith, gave a revelation to James Covill, who had been a Baptist minister for forty years. The first step in the process of becoming a Latter-day Saint, Brother Covill learned, is to accept the gospel. The Lord explained, "This is my gospel—repentance and baptism by water, and then cometh the baptism of fire and the Holy Ghost, even the Comforter, which showeth all things, and teacheth the peaceable things of the kingdom." (D&C 39:6.)

Then Brother Covill was told that accepting the gospel, he would receive a blessing greater than he had ever known. "I have prepared thee for a greater work," the Lord said, explaining, "Thou shalt preach the fulness of my gospel, which I have sent forth in these last days, the covenant which I have sent forth to recover my people, which are of the house of Israel. And it shall come to pass that power shall rest upon thee; thou shalt have great faith, and I will be with thee and go before thy face." (D&C 39:11–13.) What was said to James Covill when the Church was only nine months old applies with equal force to us now and is a remarkable and powerful reiteration of the promise made by the Savior during his earthly ministry: "Where two or three are gathered together in my name, there am I in the midst of them." (Matthew

18:20.) His pledge that he will be in our midst when two or three are gathered together in his name is a wonderful declaration of his unbounded love for us and assures us of his presence in our church services, in our individual lives, and in the intimate circles of our families.

What Jesus meant when he said his presence might be felt in the intimate circle of each of our families is, I believe, depicted in the lives of two sisters, friends of ours, who live in two widely separated stakes. One sister married out of the Church. She hoped to convert her husband and then be married and sealed in the temple. Her husband, however, has never caught the spirit nor acknowledged the truth of the gospel and has been a passive influence in the religious life of his family. Nevertheless, this woman, who has developed a lovely and spiritual personality, set a beautiful example for her family and took her children to church with her and supported them in the performance of their church duties and responsibilities. She and the children, despite what could have been a ready excuse for neglect and indifference, exemplified the admonition of Jesus when he said, "Let your light so shine before men, that [others] may see your good works, and glorify your Father which is in heaven." (Matthew 5:16.)

The second sister married a fine man who was a faithful Latter-day Saint. As the years sped by, however, they carelessly omitted what they had at first intended conscientiously to do—worship together in the name of Jesus. Although they always admired the Church and its principles, they had forgotten that they were now, in fact, the salt of the earth that had lost its savor. (Matthew 5:13.)

In a conversation about their children, the second sister asked the first, "Why have your children turned out so well and why are they so active in the Church despite the fact that you married out of the Church?" The first sister replied, "I took my children to Sunday School and sacrament meeting." Surprised, the second sister said, "I sent my children to church." And the first sister answered with greater emphasis, "Yes, but I *took* mine!" Hers was a case, as Jesus said, of "where two or three are gathered together in my name, there am I in the midst of them" (Matthew 18:20), and this can be at home or elsewhere.

On another occasion Jesus said, "I stand at the door, and knock." (Revelation 3:20.) Unless we open the door and permit him to come into our lives, he cannot enter into our midst. Mere knowledge in itself may be—but is not necessarily—power. Knowledge is not motivation. Neither is logic. The springs of human action are inherently in feelings, not in intellect, and conduct generates feelings. This is explained in the Doctrine and Covenants in these words: "Whoso receiveth you, there I will be also, for I will go before your face. I will be on your right hand and on your left, and my Spirit shall be in your hearts, and mine angels round about you, to bear you up." (D&C 84:88.)

Only in accepting our Savior and doing his will do we acquire the feelings to do right. If we break the commandments, we get feelings for that too. This explains why parents' hearts may be broken and bowed in shame because of the sins and waywardness of their sons and daughters. Puzzled and perplexed, parents sometimes say, "We brought them up to be righteous boys and girls, and our family has always been a good family. We didn't teach them to behave like this!" The children may have learned the precepts, but precepts do not necessarily furnish the will and desire to do right.

Indeed, ignorance is not the only cause of sin and deplorable conduct. Fundamental to most wrongdoing are a lack of desire, the absence of a strong motive or the right influence, and a deficiency in living the precepts. Individuals who do right and "hunger and thirst after righteousness" (Matthew 5:6) receive and keep alive through their actions the feeling to do right. Inherent in the first principles of the gospel is the "desire principle"—the desire to love God and fellowmen "with all thy heart, and with all thy soul, and with all thy mind." (Matthew 22:37.) To attain these heights, each of us must work in harmony with God's will and create a spiritual climate that will bring Jesus into the midst of our lives, and then we must continue to live "with an eye single to [his] glory." (D&C 4:5.)

This conviction is clearly demonstrated in the lives of our devoted Church members. The Apostle Paul eloquently described the process of attaining spiritual perfection in his first letter to the Thessalonians: "For our gospel came not unto you in word only, but also in power, and in the Holy Ghost, and in much assurance; as ye know what manner of men we were among you for your sake. And ye became followers of us, and of the Lord, having received the word in much affliction, with joy of the Holy Ghost: so that ye were ensamples." (1 Thessalonians 1:5–7.)

Paul rejoiced in the fact that his teachings to the Thessalonians had not been meaningless words to them, for they had listened with great interest, and what was taught to them produced a powerful desire for righteousness in their lives. He was explicit in stressing that the Holy Spirit also gave them full assurance that what was taught was true. He did not hesitate to say that his life, as well, was further proof to them of the truthfulness of the message. He was pleased that they had received the gospel message with joy and happiness, despite many hardships. Finally, he noted what must have been their crowning achievement—that they were inspiring examples to all their neighbors. He paid tribute to them when he told them that wherever he traveled, he found people telling him about their remarkable good works and faith in God. From them, the word of the Lord had extended to others everywhere, far beyond their boundaries.

Knowing and keeping the divine laws and commandments have always generated faith, righteous living, and inspiration in our people.

The early Saints in this dispensation were forced to move often, and they were troubled about how permanently they were to build their houses. When they asked the Prophet Joseph Smith about this, he told them, "Build as if you are going to stay forever." The founders of the United States—who, we believe, were divinely inspired—built the nation to endure. The leaders of the Church today never for a moment lose sight of their sacred mission. They are building for us, for those to follow, for the future, for eternity.

There is a great lesson to be learned by all of us in a careful study of our history. The success of the Church may be attributed to our faith in God and to our being led under the inspired guidance of strong and devoted leaders, never taking the shortcuts, and keeping Jesus and his divine teachings dynamically in our midst.

Wherever two or three of us are gathered together, may the Savior always be in our midst!

14

THE EXAMPLE OF JOSEPH SMITH

A timid elder from a small town, new in the mission field, hears these words: "You don't really believe that Joseph Smith story yourself." Then the door abruptly closes and he walks down the path. Suddenly he stops, retraces his steps, and knocks at the door. Though he is frightened, he speaks loudly; "You said I didn't know Joseph Smith was a prophet of God. I want you to know that I know he is, and I know he translated the Book of Mormon. I know he saw God, the Father, and His Son, Jesus Christ."

Almost halfway around the world, another young man is confronted by one who has a superior education. The young man does not have the knowledge or the training to meet the arguments. Suddenly he stands up, looks directly into the eyes of the man with the fine education, grips him by the shoulders, and says, "I haven't had much education. My father died when I was fourteen, and I have been running a ranch to help support my mother and brothers and sisters. But I know that Joseph Smith is a prophet of God."

What a lasting impact this Latter-day prophet has had upon the lives of a large segment of mankind!

A great tribute to the Prophet, written by Elder John Taylor, a witness to the events of his martyrdom, is found in section 135 of the Doctrine and Covenants:

"Joseph Smith, the Prophet and Seer of the Lord, has done more, save Jesus only, for the salvation of men in this world, than any other man that ever lived in it. In the short space of twenty years, he has brought forth the Book of Mormon, which he translated by the gift and power of God, and has been the means of publishing it on two continents; has sent the fulness of the everlasting gospel, which it contained, to the four quarters of the earth; has brought forth the revelations and commandments which compose this book of Doctrine and Covenants, and many other wise documents and instructions for the benefit of the children of men; gathered many thousands of the Latter-day Saints, founded a great city, and left a fame and name that cannot be slain. He lived great, and he died great in the eyes of God and his people; and like most of the Lord's anointed in ancient times, has sealed his mission and his works with his own blood; and so has his brother Hyrum. In life they were not divided, and in death they were not separated!" (D&C 135:3.)

From this, we learn that Joseph Smith, a prophet of God, had the most important assignment on this earth with the exception of Jesus Christ.

Joseph Smith—a man who was untrained in theology—brought forth more printed pages of scripture than the combined pages from such scripture writers as Moses, Luke, and Paul. These include his translations of the Book of Mormon and the Pearl of Great Price, the revelations found in the Doctrine and Covenants, the writings in the Pearl of Great Price, and his revisions of portions of the Bible. What came through him was clearly beyond his natural abilities.

The Prophet's great achievements did not lie alone in prophesying, in speaking, or in writing, but also in what he was. One writer wrote: "A man's true greatness is not in what he says he is, nor in what people say he is; his greatness lies in what he really is. What he really is may be determined by how he acts in unguarded moments alone with his family or close friends."[1] As President John Taylor said of Joseph Smith, "He lived great."

John M. Bernhisel, a man known for his integrity, wrote:

> Having been a boarder in General Smith's family for more than nine months, and having therefore had abundant opportunities of contemplating his character and observing his conduct, I have concluded to give you a few of my "impressions" of him.
>
> General Joseph Smith is naturally a man of strong mental powers, and is possessed of much energy and decision of character, great penetration, and a profound knowledge of human nature. He is man of calm judgment, enlarged views, and is eminently distinguished by his love of justice. He is kind and obliging, generous and benevolent, sociable and cheerful, and is possessed of a mind of a contemplative and reflective character. He is honest, frank, fearless and independent.
>
> But it is in the gentle charities of domestic life, as the tender and affectionate husband and parent, the warm and sympathizing friend, that the prominent traits of his character are revealed, and his heart is felt to be keenly alive to the kindest and softest emotions of which human nature is susceptible. . . . As a religious teacher, as well as a man, he is greatly beloved by this people.[2]

Wilford Woodruff made the following excellent and succinct observation: "I have felt to rejoice exceedingly of what I saw of Brother Joseph for in his public and private career he carried with him the Spirit of the Almighty and he manifested a greatness of soul which I have never seen in any other man."[3]

Joseph Smith's greatness of soul drew many others to him. On one occasion, after delivering a sermon to a gathering of Saints, he was arrested by the sheriff, who was in league with a group of individuals who disliked the Prophet intensely. However, the sheriff was so impressed with the Prophet after being in his presence just a few minutes that he realized he had been deceived concerning the character of the man he had arrested. He had agreed to deliver Joseph into the hands of those enemies, but when he and his prisoner approached the mob, he whipped his horse and raced past them. Stunned, they gave chase but were soon left in the distance. They stopped at an inn for the night, and the sheriff gave the Prophet the bed while he himself lay on the floor with his feet against the door and his pistol in his hand. He was determined to assure the safety of this man whom, just a few hours before, he had considered a despicable individual.[4]

It is important to be a great prophet, but one cannot be a great prophet without being a great man, "for of the abundance of the heart his mouth speaketh." (Luke 6:45.)

John A. Widtsoe, a member of the Council of the Twelve from 1921 to 1952, wrote, "Greatness is a product of many causes. It is like the mighty flowing river, fed and made possible by thousands of mountain rivulets. Even so with Joseph Smith. The reflection from innumerable facets of his character makes up the picture of Joseph Smith's greatness."[5]

Those who live as contemporaries of Joseph Smith had the advantage of knowing him personally, but we who live a century and a half after his martyrdom are not without advantage. We have the advantage of perspective. Time has a way of supporting those who are truly great and exposing those who would fain greatness. The Lord called Joseph not just to be an example and guide to those of his own day but to benefit, through his teachings, those who would come after.

Elder Widtsoe noted that Joseph Smith had four qualities that made him great and were "the cornerstones of his character: (1) He had unchanging faith and trust in God. (2) He loved truth. (3). He was humble. (4). He loved his fellowmen. These qualities always lead to greatness. Without them there is no true greatness.

"Doubt did not belong to Joseph Smith's nature. The Prophet's faith in God—in His existence, reality, and relationship to man—was superb. Joseph took God at his word, as in the First Vision."[6]

Joseph Smith lacked knowledge, but through prayer he approached God in faith, and an answer was given to him. (See James 1:5.) Throughout his life he took counsel with the Almighty and did not try to act alone upon his own judgment. He accepted the responsibility of restoring the kingdom of God on earth. In spite of brutal treatment and heartbreaking defeats, his mind was ever active. He had faith and trust in the Lord.

Joseph knew only one direction: forward. At the time of his death he was still building Nauvoo into a major city, devoting energy to his campaign for the presidency of the United States, and organizing explorers to seek out a location in the West were the Saints could move and become a mighty people. He asked his followers to do nothing he would not do himself.

Because of his faith, the Prophet served even when it was not convenient. He also asked others who followed the Lord to serve when they were in the most trying circumstances. Brigham Young, Heber C. Kimball, and Wilford Woodruff did not find it inconvenient to return to Far West in fulfillment of a prophecy the Prophet made a year before, in 1839, when he was in the hands of bitter enemies. But Brigham Young would not allow a prophecy to be unfulfilled. Despite sickness among themselves and their families, and having to leave their loved ones in the most dire circumstances, the faithful apostles traveled many miles to return to Far West and then took leave for their missions. These sacrifices and manifestations of faith and obedience brought forth great blessings to the kingdom. The apostles converted many thousands in England who had been praying for the truth.

With his great faith and trust in God, Joseph had an insurmountable optimism. He knew the truth, and the truth made him free—free from fear, free from doubt, and free from pessimism. He said, "If I were sunk in the lowest pit of Nova Scotia, with the Rocky Mountains piled on me, I would hang on, exercise faith, and keep up good courage, and I would come out on top."[7]

Why was Joseph able to be cheerful, hopeful, and pleasant, and engage in fun-filled activities? He wrote: "Now, what do we hear in the gospel which we have received? A voice of gladness! A voice of mercy from heaven; and a voice of truth out of the earth; glad tidings for the dead; a voice of gladness for the living and the dead; glad tidings of great joy. . . .

"Brethren, shall we not go on in so great a cause? Go forward and not backward. Courage, brethren; and on, on to the victory! Let your hearts rejoice, and be exceedingly glad. . . .

"Let the mountains shout for joy, and all ye valleys cry aloud; . . . and let all the sons of God shout for joy!" (D&C 128:19, 22–23.)

The Prophet loved truth. His story began with his petition for truth, which led to the First Vision. Truth made him fearless. He had a lionlike courage. He could not exchange truth for popular approval. When the people of Palmyra held a mass meeting at the time the Book of Mormon was being printed and passed a resolution against his venture, his reply was to guard the manuscript of the book more carefully.[8]

There was no retreat from truth. He published the Book of Mormon and went on to organize a church that challenged the popular errors and superstitions of the centuries.

Not only did he love truth, but he also had a remarkable ability to teach truth. Brigham Young said, "The excellency of the glory of the character of Brother Joseph Smith was that he could reduce heavenly things to the understanding of the infinite. When he preached to the people—revealed the things of God, the will of God, the plan of salvation, the purposes of Jehovah, the relation in which we stand to him and all the heavenly beings, he reduced his teachings to the capacity of every man, woman, and child, making them as plain as a well-defined pathway. This should have convinced every person that ever heard him of his divine authority and power, for no other man was able to teach as he could, and no person can reveal the things of God, but by the revelations of Jesus Christ."[9]

Elder Charles W. Penrose was impressed with the Prophet's ability to assist others in obtaining knowledge from God: "He was enabled to instruct the inhabitants of the earth how they could obtain the Holy Ghost so they could obtain a knowledge of his existence through this heavenly gift so they might be guided in his ways and know that they were walking in his paths."[10]

Joseph was a humble man. He recognized that he was only an instrument in God's hands. He took no glory to himself. He told the Saints, "I am a man and they must not expect me to be perfect. If they expect perfection from me, I should expect it from them, but if they would bear with my infirmities and the infirmities of the brethren, I would likewise bear with their infirmities."[11]

Joseph was completely honest. He honestly and openly made public his weaknesses. He honestly and openly expressed love. He honestly and openly expressed remorse.

Contrary to the will of the Lord, Joseph allowed Martin Harris to take the first 116 pages of the Book of Mormon manuscript that had been translated. When Martin lost them and the Lord chastised Joseph severely, Joseph made no attempt to hide his error or the Lord's rebuke. The account is in sections 3 and 10 of the Doctrine and Covenants and is readily available for all the world to read. He did not try to hide his weaknesses. He was more concerned with helping others by example than he was with improving his own image or building his own ego.

On one occasion he characterized himself: "I am like a huge, rough stone rolling down from a high mountain; and the only polishing I get is when some corner gets rubbed off by coming in contact with something else, . . . [such as] religious bigotry, priestcraft, lawyer-craft, doctor-craft, lying editors, . . . mobs, blasphemy, . . . and corrupt men and women—all hell knocking off a corner here and a corner there. Thus I will become smooth and polished shaft in the quiver of the Almighty, who will give me dominion over all."[12]

The Prophet loved his fellowmen. He did not hesitate to tell them so or to show his love by his acts. The end of a letter to Jared Carter reads: "I love your soul, and the souls of the children of men, and pray all I can for the salvation of all."[13]

Because of his love for his fellowmen, Joseph never missed

an opportunity to preach the gospel. He was almost certainly a missionary. When he visited Washington, D.C., he told the president of the United States about the gospel. While in prison, he taught the gospel to guards. Love for his fellowmen included exceedingly great love for his family, his wife, his children, his parents, and his brothers and sisters.

Joseph's interest in others and his concern for their welfare was felt by nearly everybody. He enjoyed wrestling. Even as an adult he frequently played catch, pulled sticks, and engaged in similar contests with young people. He often told jokes, to the amusement of his companions, and moved upon the same plain of the humblest and poorest of his friends. To him there were no strangers.[14]

Joseph had a capacity to forgive, as is displayed in a letter he wrote to W. W. Phelps. After Brother Phelps had signed an affidavit that led to the arrest of Joseph and resulted in much suffering for the Saints, Joseph wrote to him: "It is true, that we have suffered much in consequence of your behavior—the cup of gall, already full enough for mortals to drink, was indeed filled to overflowing when you turned against us. One with whom we had oft taken sweet counsel together, and enjoyed many refreshing seasons from the Lord—'had it been an enemy, we could have borne it.' . . . However, the cup has been drunk, the will of our Father has been done, and we are yet alive, for which we thank the Lord. . . . I shall be happy once again to give you the right hand of fellowship, and rejoice over the returning prodigal. . . . 'Come on, dear brother, since the war has past, / For friends at first are friends again at last.'"[15]

Brother Phelps went on to be rebaptized and was a faithful member of the Church.

Writing in his journal in August 1842, the Prophet

revealed his deep love for his wife, Emma: "With what unspeakable delight, and what transports of joy swelled by bosom, when I took by the hand, on that night, my beloved Emma—she that was my wife, even the wife of my youth, and the choice of my heart. Many were the reverberations of my mind when I contemplated for a moment the many scenes we had been called to pass through, the fatigues and the toils, the sorrows and sufferings, and the joys and consolations, from time to time, which had strewed our paths and crowned our board."[16]

Once when he was in prison for an extended time, Joseph wrote to her: "My dear Emma, I very well know your toils and sympathize with you. If God will spare my life once more to have the privilege of taking care of you, I will ease your care and endeavor to comfort your heart."[17]

Six of the eleven children of the Prophet and his wife—five natural children and one adopted son—did not survive infancy. Four natural sons and an adopted daughter lived to maturity. Emma gave birth to her last child at the age of forty, five months after the Prophet's death. He loved his children and recorded many activities with them, such as these: "After dinner I rode out in company with my wife and children." "Enjoyed myself at home with my family, all day, it being Christmas." "Remained at home and had great joy with my family."

Joseph had great love for his parents. "Words and language are inadequate the gratitude that I own to God for having given me so honorable a parentage," he wrote. "I love my father and his memory; and the memory of his noble deeds rests with ponderous weight upon my mind, and many of his kind and parental words to me are written on the tablet of my heart. . . . My mother also is one of the noblest and the best of all women. May God grant to prolong her days and mine, that we may live to enjoy each other's society long."[18]

Joseph's relationship with his brother Hyrum was like that of David and Jonathan: "I could pray in my heart that all my brethren were like unto my beloved brother Hyrum, who possesses the mildness of a lamb, and the integrity of a Job, and in short, the meekness and humility of Christ; and I love him with a love that is stronger than death, for I never had occasion to rebuke him, nor him me."[19]

This love and appreciation also extended to his other brothers, two of whom preceded him in death. He wrote:

"Alvin, my oldest brother—I remember well the pangs of sorrow that swelled my youthful bosom and almost burst my tender heart when he died. He was the oldest and the noblest of my father's family. He was one of the noblest of the sons of men. . . . In him there was no guile. He lived without spot from the time he was a child . . . and when he died the angel of the Lord visited him in his last moments."[20]

"My brother, Don Carlos Smith, . . . also was a noble boy; I never knew any fault in him. . . . He was lovely, a good-natured, a kind-hearted and a virtuous and a faithful, upright child; and where his soul goes, let mine go also."[21]

It seems appropriate that Joseph received revelations from God and the sealing power to assure that family life would be continued forever eternally. It must have eased the pain of separation from Alvin to know that in the future, all of the Smith family could again be reunited. The Prophet Joseph has brought comfort and joy to numerous faithful who also have known the pain and heartbreak of separation from loved ones. The Lord Jesus Christ has always placed primary emphasis on the home and family, and his servant, Joseph Smith, demonstrated this in his personal behavior. Joseph did not ignore, but joyfully accepted his responsibility as a family member.

Yes, the Prophet truly had greatness of soul. The four cornerstones of his character—faith, love of truth and humanity, humility, and love of his fellowmen—make him the epitome of the whole, well-rounded man.

NOTES

1. Leon Hartshorn, *Joseph Smith, Prophet of the Restoration* (Salt Lake City: Deseret Book Company, 1970), p. 38.
2. *History of the Church [HC]* 6:468.
3. *Journal of Discourses [JD]* 7:176.
4. *HC* 1:88–89.
5. "I Have a Question," *Improvement Era,* December 1948, p. 809.
6. Ibid.
7. Quoted in John Henry Evans, *Joseph Smith, An American Prophet,* Classics in Mormon Literature ed. (Salt Lake City: Deseret Book Company, 1989), p. 9.
8. *HC* 1:76.
9. *JD* 8:206.
10. *JD* 23:348–49
11. *HC* 5:181.
12. *HC* 5:401.
13. *HC* 1:339.
14. Leonard J. Arrington, "Human Qualities of Joseph Smith the Prophet," *Ensign,* January 1971, pp. 36–37.
15. *HC* 4:163–64.
16. *HC* 5:107.
17. Quoted in Church section, *Deseret News,* April 17, 1968, p. 3.
18. *HC* 5:126.
19. *HC* 2:338.
20. *HC* 5:126.
21. *HC* 5:127.

PART TWO

Finding Peace within Ourselves

*To be spiritually minded
is life and peace.*

Romans 8:6

DEEP ROOTS

Recently on the island of Molokai in the Hawaiian Islands, Sister Wirthlin and I passed by two very large trees that the wind had blown down and uprooted. These huge trees had extremely shallow roots. I wondered if they would have survived the winds and storms if their roots had been deeper. Relatively mild gusts of wind blow some trees down. Graceful palm trees, for example, are lovely to look at but will not stand up in a heavy wind because they are not well anchored. Contrast this with giant oak trees, which have deep root systems that can extend two and a half times their height. Such trees are rarely blown down regardless of how violent the storms may be.

Faithful members of the Church should be like oak trees and extend deep roots into the fertile soil of the fundamental principles of the gospel. We should understand and live by the simple, basic truths and not complicate them. Our foundations should be solid and deep rooted so we can withstand the winds of temptation, false doctrine, adversity, and the onslaught of the adversary without being swayed or uprooted. Members whose roots are only at the surface of the gospel need to sink them deeper until they reach the bedrock below the soft topsoil.

Spiritual nourishment is just as important as a balanced

diet to keep us strong and healthy. We nourish ourselves spiritually by partaking of the sacrament weekly, reading the scriptures daily, praying in personal and family prayer daily, and performing temple work regularly. Our spiritual strengths are like batteries; they need to be charged and recharged.

I wish to review with you a few core principles of the gospel into which our spiritual roots should sink deeply. Most important is the reality of our Heavenly Father; his Son, Jesus Christ; and the Holy Ghost.

Our Heavenly Father is the father of our spirits and of the entire human race; we are his offspring, his sons and daughters. We have inherited divine characteristics from him. Because of his love for his children, he provided a plan for us to progress and reach our highest potential and return to his presence. The Prophet Joseph Smith taught, "God himself, finding he was in the midst of spirits and glory, because he was more intelligent, saw proper to institute laws whereby the rest could have a privilege to advance like himself."[1]

Jesus Christ is infinitely more than a great teacher and philosopher. He is the Firstborn Son of God, the Only Begotten Son in the flesh, the Savior and Redeemer of all mankind. He *accepted* the Father's great plan of happiness, saying, "Father, thy will be done, and the glory be thine forever." (Moses 4:2.) The Father's plan gave us our agency to choose right or wrong, good or evil so we can learn, develop, and progress. As part of the plan, Jesus offered to atone for the sins of all mankind and bear the suffering for those sins, satisfying the law of justice, if the sinners repent. Otherwise, they have to suffer and pay the penalty for their transgressions.

He also offered his mortal life, was crucified, and became the first to be resurrected, making possible the literal resurrection of all of our Father's children. He created this earth

116

under his Father's direction as a place for us to live in mortality and prove whether we would be obedient and "do all things whatsoever the Lord [our] God shall command." (Abraham 3:25.) He also created innumerable other worlds. He is our Mediator with the Father and our Exemplar in all things. His loving kindness toward us is beyond our comprehension. He stands at the head of his church, which bears his name, and directs it through his prophets.

The Lord Jesus Christ is the Rock of our salvation. He said in the Sermon on the Mount: "Whosoever heareth these sayings of mine, and doeth them, I will liken him unto a wise man, which built his house upon a rock: And the rain descended, and the floods came, and the winds blew, and beat upon that house; and if fell not: for it was founded upon a rock.

"And every one that heareth these sayings of mine, and doeth them not, shall be likened unto a foolish man, which built his house upon the sand: And the rain descended, and the floods came, and the winds blew, and beat upon that house; and it fell." (Matthew 7:24–27.)

To the Saints in this dispensation, he said, "Do good; let earth and hell combine against you, for if ye are built upon my rock, they cannot prevail." (D&C 6:34.)

The Holy Ghost is the third member of the Godhead. As the Prophet Joseph Smith taught, "The Father has a body of flesh and bones as tangible as man's; the Son also; but the Holy Ghost has not a body of flesh and bones, but is a personage of Spirit." (D&C 130:22.) He is a witness and testifier of the truth of the gospel. He is a revelator and teacher who conveys information to our spirits with far more certainty than is possible by our natural senses. He can guide us in every choice and decision and will never deceive or mislead us. He is a comforter who brings peace to our souls in times of need.

Just as real is one who would prevent us from becoming rooted to God and his truths. Two of his names are Lucifer and Satan. He is the adversary of our Heavenly Father and Jesus Christ and of everything that is good. He rejected the Father's plan in premortal life, saying, "Send me, I will be thy son, and I will redeem all mankind, that one soul shall not be lost, and surely I will do it; wherefore give me thine honor."

The Father then said: "Because that Satan rebelled against me, and sought to destroy the agency of man, which I, the Lord God, had given him, also, that I should give unto him mine own power; by the power of mine Only Begotten, I cause that he should be cast down; and he became Satan, yea, even the devil, the father of all lies, to deceive and to blind men, and to lead them captive at his will, even as many as would not hearken unto my voice." (Moses 4:1, 3–4.)

From that time forward, Satan has led the forces of evil in a battle for the souls of men in his attempt to frustrate the plan of salvation. We learn from the Book of Mormon prophet Moroni that "all things which are good cometh of God; and that which is evil cometh of the devil; for the devil is an enemy unto God, and fighteth against him continually, and inviteth and enticeth to sin, and to do that which is evil continually.

"But behold, that which is of God inviteth and enticeth to do good continually; wherefore, every thing which inviteth and enticeth to do good, and to love God, and to serve him, is inspired of God. . . .

"For behold, the Spirit of Christ is given to every man, that he may know good from evil; . . . for every thing which inviteth to do good, and to persuade to believe in Christ, is sent forth by the power and gift of Christ; wherefore ye may know with a perfect knowledge it is of God.

"But whatsoever thing persuadeth men to do evil, and believe not in Christ, and deny him, and serve not God, then ye may know with a perfect knowledge it is of the devil; for after this manner doth the devil work, for he persuadeth no man to do good, no, not one; neither do his angels; neither do they who subject themselves unto him." (Moroni 7:12–13, 16–17.)

The sins of corruption, dishonesty, strife, contention, and other evils in this world are not here by chance. They are evidences of the relentless campaign of Satan and those who follow him. He uses every tool and device available to him to deceive, confuse, and mislead. He has many followers who do anything for money without regard for the effects of their misdeeds.

Another core principle is moral purity. One of the most pervasive deceptions in recent years is the notion that immorality is normal and acceptable and has no negative consequences. In truth, immorality is the underlying cause of much suffering and many other problems that are prevalent today, including rampant disease, abortion, broken families, families without fathers, and mothers who themselves are children. President Ezra Taft Benson said, "The plaguing sin of this generation is sexual immorality."[2] The Lord said "Thou shalt not . . . commit adultery, . . . nor do anything like unto it." (D&C 59:6.) That means we are to avoid abnormal sexual behavior, including fornication, homosexual behavior, child molestation, or any other perversion of God's plan of happiness.

A gospel principle that provides spiritual and physical strength is the Word of Wisdom. For many years after the Prophet Joseph Smith received this revelation in 1833, people deceived themselves into believing they could ignore or violate this law of health with impunity. I believe the Lord inspired President Heber J. Grant to emphasize it frequently and forcefully to counter the advertising that was becoming increasingly sophisticated and persuasive during his time. Today, medical science has proven that tobacco and other such addictive substances are poisons and are harmful to the human body.

We can reach out to others in missionary service in response to the Savior's injunction to "go . . . into all the world, and preach the gospel to every creature." Mark 16:15.) The Lord used a harvest analogy when he instructed the early Saints to proclaim the gospel. He said, "Behold, the field is white already to harvest; therefore, whoso desireth to reap, let him thrust in his sickle with his might, and reap while the day lasts, that he may treasure up for his soul everlasting salvation in the kingdom of God." (D&C 6:3.) That is our sacred privilege and obligation.

The field is still white and ready to harvest. Latter-day Saints remain a small percentage of the world's population. "For there are many yet on the earth among all sects, parties, and denominations . . . who are only kept from the truth because they know not where to find it." (D&C 123:12.) In proclaiming the gospel, we need to be sensitive to the feelings of others, remembering that "we claim the privilege of worshiping Almighty God according to the dictates of our own conscience, and allow all men the same privilege, let them worship how, where, or what they may." (Article of Faith 11.)

Missionaries labor diligently to teach and baptize those who accept the gospel. In the process, their own testimonies become deeply rooted. Missionary service provides the finest foundation possible for young people as they move into adulthood. The deep roots they sink into the gospel will sustain them for a lifetime and for all eternity. The Church needs more missionaries, many more, including couples, to fulfill its charge to proclaim the gospel "unto all nations, kindreds, tongues and people." (D&C 42:58.)

God has revealed everything necessary for our salvation. We should teach and dwell on the things that have been revealed and avoid delving into so-called mysteries. My counsel to teachers in the Church, whether they instruct in wards, stakes, Church institutions of higher learning, institutes of religion, seminaries, or as parents in their homes, is to base their teachings on the scriptures and the words of latter-day prophets.

We should follow Paul's counsel to the Ephesians: "Be no more . . . tossed to and fro, and carried about with every wind of doctrine." (Ephesians 4:14.) The winds of false doctrine that are blowing today both outside and a few within the Church are far more dangerous to the ultimate salvation of mankind than are earthquakes, hurricanes, typhoons, volcanic eruptions, and other natural disasters. These winds can uproot people if their roots are not firmly anchored to the rock of our salvation, which is the teachings of the gospel of Jesus Christ.

We, as a people, are to live our religion and its principles and follow the leadership of our prophet, seer, and revelator regardless of what the world does. We should strive always to be obedient to our Heavenly Father and Jesus Christ, and should keep in mind these words of the Savior: "I, the Lord, am bound when ye do what I say, but when ye do not what I say, ye have no promise." (D&C 82:10.)

The Lord has reserved America as the place for the restoration of his church. For this land to achieve its full potential, its citizens must remain rooted firmly in the principles that made it great. The enemies of God are attacking the core foundations of this land. The Lord's law for it is declared in the Book of Mormon, where we read that this land is a "land of promise, . . . which the Lord had preserved for a righteous people. . . . And whatsoever nation shall possess it shall serve God, or they shall be swept off." (Ether 2:7, 9.)

As we understand and live the fundamental principles, we will develop unshakable testimonies and convictions of their truth that will keep us from ever being swayed or uprooted.

Our Heavenly Father has endowed us with hearts of courage and faith, with strong wills and the ability to understand and to see clearly the difference between right and wrong, good and evil. He mercifully has clothed each member with the gift of the Holy Ghost, which gives us insight and personal power.

Even though the tasks of life become heavy, and although sorrow thrusts a drooping burden upon us, the light that emanates from our Savior beckons us on, undismayed. A righteous self-discipline can and will rule our lives.

The Church of Jesus Christ of Latter-day Saints does not and will not in any way compromise its position, and never at any time or place does it falter, hesitate, or show any reluctance to bear unwavering testimony to the divinity of Jesus Christ. Let us not forget the two giant trees we observed in Molokai whose roots were not strong or deep enough for the trees to withstand the heavy winds that destroyed them. I bear testimony that we can find peace, security, and joy and happiness in the principles of the gospel.

NOTES

1. *Teachings of the Prophet Joseph Smith,* p. 354.
2. *The Teachings of Ezra Taft Benson* (Salt Lake City: Bookcraft, 1988), p. 277.

16

Spiritual Bonfires of Testimony

Many years ago, large packs of wolves roamed the country-side in Ukraine, making travel in that part of the world very dangerous. These wolf packs were fearless. They were not intimidated by people or by any of the weapons available at that time. The only thing that seemed to frighten them was fire. Consequently, travelers who found themselves away from cities developed the practice of building a large bonfire and keeping it burning through the night. As long as the fire burned brightly, the wolves stayed away. But if the fire burned out, the wolves would move in for an attack. Travelers understood that building and maintaining a bonfire was not just a matter of convenience or comfort; it was a matter of survival.[1]

We do not have to protect ourselves from wolf packs as we travel the road of life today, but, in a spiritual sense, we do face the devious wolves of Satan in the form of temptation, evil, and sin. We live in dangerous times when the ravenous wolves roam the spiritual countryside in search of those who may be weak in faith or feeble in their conviction.

In his first epistle, Peter described our "adversary the devil, as a roaring lion, [that] walketh about, seeking whom he may devour." (1 Peter 5:8.) The Lord told the Prophet Joseph Smith, "Enemies prowl around thee like wolves for the blood of the lamb." (D&C 122:6.) We are all vulnerable to attack.

However, we can fortify ourselves with the protection provided by a burning testimony that, like a bonfire, has been built adequately and maintained carefully.

Unfortunately, some in the Church may believe sincerely that their testimony is a raging bonfire when it really is little more than the faint flickering of a candle. Their faithfulness has more to do with habit than holiness, and their pursuit of personal righteousness almost always takes a back seat to their pursuit of personal interests and pleasure. With such a feeble light of testimony for protection, these travelers on life's highways are easy prey for the wolves of the adversary.

The Savior understood that many of his followers would struggle under the rigors of true discipleship; consequently, he taught them how to build burning testimonies. The night before his crucifixion, he shared the feast of the Passover with his twelve beloved apostles, most of whom had been with him throughout his ministry. At one point during this sacred evening, he looked upon Peter, his senior apostle and loyal friend. Knowing what would be required of Peter after the Ascension, the Lord said: "Simon, Simon, behold, Satan hath desired to have you, that he may sift you as wheat: But I have prayed for thee, that thy faith fail not: and when thou art converted, strengthen thy brethren." (Luke 22:31–32.)

Imagine for a moment that you are Peter. Three years ago a holy stranger invited you to set aside your fishing boat and nets, your means of support for yourself and your family, and then asked you to follow him. You did so without hesitation, and for three years you have continued to follow and to love and support and sustain him. You have seen him confound the wise, comfort the weary and the afflicted, heal the sick, and raise the dead to life. You have seen him conquer evil spirits and calm the troubled seas; and for a few minutes, at

124

least, you even walked on the water toward him. You were at his side when Moses and Elias appeared to him; you saw him transfigured before your very eyes. You have committed your entire life to him. And now he questions you by instructing you to strengthen your brethren—"when thou art converted."

Peter was surprised. He assured the Lord, "I am ready to go with thee, both into prison, and to death." (Luke 22:33.) But Jesus knew and understood. He was not condemning Peter for a lack of conviction; Peter demonstrated his conviction during the Lord's arrest. Rather, the Savior was telling Peter what he needed to do when his testimony became more secure.

As he knew Peter, the Lord understands us today when our testimonies may not be the brightly burning bonfire we may think they are or want them to be. Perhaps in some cases, that testimony is constructed unwisely, built on a social foundation of programs and personalities instead of the sure rock of personal revelation. Or perhaps we have allowed our testimony to flicker gradually through disuse and spiritual complacency. Regardless of the reason, the Savior lovingly urges us to come unto him and become strengthened in him. Said he to Moroni: "If men come unto me I will show unto them their weakness. I give unto men weakness that they may be humble; . . . for if they humble themselves before me, and have faith in me, then will I make weak things become strong unto them." (Ether 12:27.)

Some people are weak in their faith and testimonies but are not even aware of how precarious their situation is. Many of them likely would be offended at the suggestion. They raise their right hand to sustain Church leaders and then murmur and complain when a decision does not square with their way of thinking. They claim to be obedient to God's commandments but do not feel at all uncomfortable about purchasing food at the store on Sunday and then asking the Lord to bless it. Some say they would give their lives for the Lord, yet they refuse to serve in the nursery.

The Savior spoke explicitly about people who "draw near [him] with their mouth, and with their lips do honour [him], but have removed their heart far from [him]." (Isaiah 29:13.) His words were: "Not every one that saith unto me, Lord, Lord, shall enter into the kingdom of heaven; but he that doeth the will of my Father which is in heaven. Many will say to me in that day, Lord, Lord, have we not prophesied in thy name? and in thy name have cast out devils? and in thy name done many wonderful works? And then will I profess unto them, I never knew you: depart from me, ye that work iniquity." (Matthew 7:21–23.)

None would want to hear the Lord speak such disappointing words. That is why we need to do everything in our power to be certain our spiritual bonfire of testimony is burning brightly enough to keep the wolves of darkness away. We can always use more dry kindling. As the Apostle Paul taught, each of us has "come short of the glory of God." (Romans 3:23.) None of us has progressed so far in this life that we do not need to continually fortify our testimonies.

I offer three suggestions that will fan the flame of personal testimony as a protection against the wolves of evil that are prowling all around us to threaten our spiritual security.

First, our testimonies must be built upon a solid foundation of faith in the Lord, Jesus Christ.

Even though we may enjoy the fellowship of the Saints and may have strong feelings about the inspired programs of the Church, we must remember that we have only one sure anchor for our souls. This is stated in the words of the prophet Helaman, when he taught his sons:

126

"And now, my sons, remember, remember that it is upon the rock of our Redeemer, who is Christ, the Son of God, that ye must build your foundation; that when the devil shall send forth his mighty winds, yea, his shafts in the whirlwind, yea, when all his hail and his mighty storm shall beat upon you, it shall have no power over you to drag you down to the gulf of misery and endless wo, because of the rock upon which ye are built, which is a sure foundation, a foundation whereon if men build they cannot fall." (Helaman 5:12.)

Perhaps you are one of the members of the Church whose first contact with the gospel came through the beautiful music of the Tabernacle Choir. Maybe your life was blessed by the Church welfare program when you followed prophetic counsel to store food and other necessities. These are marvelous, inspired aspects of the Church that God has provided to help bring his children to Christ. However, they are implements and not ends in themselves. The ultimate focus of our devotion must properly be our Heavenly Father and his Beloved Son, Jesus Christ.

We often hear of members who have separated themselves from the Church because a leader, teacher, or member has said or done something to offend them. Others have had their faith shaken when the Brethren have taken a stand with which they disagree. I wonder about the faith of such people and whether it is grounded in a testimony of the Lord, Jesus Christ, or merely based on their own ideas and perceptions of what the Church and its members should be.

Scripture teaches us: "Trust in the Lord with all thine heart; and lean not unto thine own understanding." (Proverbs 3:5.) In his moving prayer recorded in the seventeenth chapter of John, the Savior taught this profound truth: "This is life eternal, that they might know thee the only true God, and

Jesus Christ, whom thou hast sent." (John 17:3.) Building a testimony on the foundation of a sincere, personal relationship with our Heavenly Father and Jesus Christ, and on our faith in them, should be our highest priority.

Second, we must repent humbly and sincerely.

Few things extinguish the fervor of the Holy Spirit in the heart of any individual more quickly than does sin. It dulls the spiritual senses, diminishes confidence and personal security, and separates the sinner from the Savior. One who carries the burden of unrepented sins is more likely to rationalize additional disobedience. The more sin is rationalized, the greater the possibility of destruction by Satan's wolves.

Few would argue the potential spiritual risk of major sins such as murder or marital infidelity. But what about the person who uses employer's time to complete personal projects, the person who sneaks into a pornographic movie, the student who cheats at school, the person who criticizes others unfairly, or the parent who thinks family home evening is a good idea—for someone else?

The simple fact is this: anything that does not draw us closer to God takes us away from him. There is no middle ground, no foggy gray area where we can sin a little without suffering spiritual decline. That is why we must repent and come to Christ daily on submissive knees so that we can prevent our bonfires of testimony from being snuffed out by sin.

Third, we must follow the example of the Savior.

In any pursuit and under any condition, we can ask ourselves what Jesus would do and then determine our own course accordingly. For example, what sort of home teacher would the Savior be? Would he visit any family without a message? Or would he minister to his families like the good shepherd that he is, with constant watch care and loving kindness? Deep in our hearts we know what kind of home teacher Jesus would be, just as we know what kind of bishop, teacher, Primary leader, clerk, or youth adviser he would be. Even though we could never in this life measure up completely to his standard of excellence, our attempt to do so will lead us to do far better than otherwise.

We can apply the same principle to other pursuits. What sort of parent would Jesus be? What sort of neighbor, employer, employee, student, or friend? If we live our lives to conform as nearly as possible to the pattern the Savior has set, our testimonies will be fortified continually and our spiritual bonfires will never be reduced to embers.

We live in perilous times. The influence of Satan often appears to be unchecked and overwhelming. Remember the promise God has given to those who build and maintain bonfires of testimony to counter the wolves that threaten us: "Fear thou not; for I am with thee: be not dismayed; for I am thy God: I will strengthen thee; yea, I will . . . uphold thee with the right hand of my righteousness." (Isaiah 41:10.)

The strength of the Church lies in the depth and vitality of the personal testimonies of its members. Firm, secure testimonies will be the difference between faithfulness and disaffection. In order for us to enjoy a happy, rewarding, spiritual life, we must make sure our testimonies are built upon the foundation of faith in Jesus Christ, humble and sincere repentance, and following the example of the Savior.

NOTE

1. See Mary Pratt Parish, "Guardians of the Covenant," *Ensign,* May 1972, p. 25.

17

SEEKING THE GOOD

A key document of the restoration of the gospel is a letter the Prophet Joseph Smith wrote in reply to a request of John Wentworth, editor of a Chicago newspaper. In it, the Prophet wrote a "sketch of the rise, progress, persecution, and faith of the Latter-day Saints."[1] It apparently was the first published account of principal events that occurred in the thirty-six-year period after the Prophet's birth. The last section of the letter, the Articles of Faith, is a concise statement of fundamental beliefs of the Church. The thirteenth article concludes: "If there is anything virtuous, lovely, or of good report or praiseworthy, we seek after these things." (A of F 1:13.)

The word *seek* means to go in search of, try to discover, try to acquire. It requires an active, assertive approach to life. For example, Abraham "sought for the blessings of the fathers . . . and to be a greater follower of righteousness." (Abraham 1:2.) This is the opposite of passively waiting for something good to come to us, with no effort on our part.

We can fill our lives with good, leaving no room for anything else. We have so much good from which to choose that we need never to partake of evil. Elder Richard L. Evans declared: "There is evil in the world. These is also good. It is for us to learn and choose between the two; increase in self-discipline, in competence, in kindness; to keep going—

putting one foot in front of the other—one day, one hour, one moment, one task at a time."[2]

If we seek things that are virtuous and lovely, we surely will find them. Conversely, if we seek for evil, we will find that also. Lucifer understands how to tempt and drag many of our Heavenly Father's children down to where he and his followers are. He rebelled and was cast out; he wants to make us as miserable as he is. (See 2 Nephi 2:18.)

My message may be the opposite of the worldly message of Satan's fallacy. Nephi described it when he wrote: "Many . . . shall say: Eat, drink, and be merry, for tomorrow we die; and it shall be well with us. . . . Nevertheless, fear God—he will justify in committing a little sin; yea, lie a little, take the advantage of one . . . ; there is no harm in this; and do all these things, for tomorrow we die; and if it so be that we are guilty, God will beat us with a few stripes, and at last we shall be saved in the kingdom of God." (2 Nephi 28:7–8.)

Though we live *in* the world, we must not be *of* the world. For members of the Church, seeking the good is more than a lofty ideal. It is an obligation we accepted when we entered the waters of baptism; we renew it each time we partake of the sacrament. We must remember: "The Lord cannot look upon sin with the least degree of allowance; nevertheless, he that repents and does the commandments of the Lord shall be forgiven." (D&C 1:31–32.)

We can seek to strengthen our families and can foster peace and happiness in our homes, making them a safe haven from the cares and woes about us. By example, parents can teach children to be kind, considerate, respectful, and supportive of one another and to avoid strife and contention. Occasionally, family members treat each other with less courtesy and kindness than they do acquaintances or even strangers. Family members do have differences that can cause friction, but they should reserve their most tender affection for those who are closest to them: their spouse, parents, brothers and sisters. The true greatness of a person, in my view, is evident in the way he or she treats those toward whom courtesy and kindness may not be required.

We can seek to be good neighbors. In most cases, those who are good neighbors will have good neighbors. Being a good neighbor means doing more than offering a thoughtful gesture from time to time on a holiday or crisis. It means striving continuously to build and maintain genuine friendship. We react quickly in an emergency. For example, when our neighbor's car caught on fire, everyone who saw the flames immediately rushed out to help. Do we respond as well when the need is less urgent but perhaps very important?

We can seek to provide selfless service because of the love we have for our fellowmen. The Savior placed such love second only to love for God when he said: "Thou shalt love the Lord thy God with all thy heart, and with all thy soul, and with all thy mind. This is the first and great commandment. And the second is like unto it, Thou shalt love thy neighbour as thyself. On these two commandments hang all the law and the prophets." (Matthew 22:37–40.)

Regarding these two commandments, we read in the book of First John: "If a man say, I love God, and hateth his brother, he is a liar: for he that loveth not his brother whom he hath seen, how can he love God whom he hath not seen? And this commandment have we from him, That he who loveth God love his brother also." (1 John 4:20–21.)

Serving others should become a natural part of the life of every follower of the Savior. When we subordinate personal interests out of love and give of ourselves with no thought of receiving in return, we are moving toward becoming true disciples. We have been commanded to care for the poor among us. The Lord said: "Remember in all things the poor and the needy, the sick and the afflicted, for he that doeth not these things, the same is not my disciple." (D&C 52:40.)

We should seek to become self-reliant, as far as possible, rather than depend on someone else to provide for us. Some people seem to have the notion that we have a right to everything in life without making any effort to produce it ourselves. Many believe the government and others should take care of us: they think they should provide food, health care, and housing. Of course, society must care for some of its people, but the general population should get away from the idea of depending on the government for things they can provide for themselves and their families.

We should seek to be happy and cheerful and not allow Satan to overcome us with discouragement, despair, or depression. President Benson said, "Of all people, we as Latter-day Saints should be the most optimistic and the least pessimistic."[3] Where sin is the cause of unhappiness, we need to repent and return to a righteous life, because "wickedness never was happiness." (Alma 41:10.)

I believe happiness comes from a clear conscience and from being without guile or deception. It means avoiding jealousy and envy. It means cultivating peace in our homes and enjoying the peace in our hearts that righteousness brings. It comes from a knowledge and assurance, given by the Spirit, that the life we are pursuing is in accord with God's will and is acceptable to him. The Prophet Joseph's oft-quoted statement remains in force: "Happiness is the object and design of our existence; and will be the end thereof, if we pursue the path that leads to it; and this path is virtue, uprightness, faithfulness, holiness, and keeping all the commandments of God."[4] We need not feel depressed or discouraged about conditions in the world, for the Lord will help us find the good that will lead us to happiness.

In a day when broadcasters and publishers have rather free access into our homes, we must seek clean, uplifting entertainment, on television and videos and in movies, magazines, books, and other printed material. We should be very selective and choose only those things that meet the test of being virtuous, lovely, of good report, or praiseworthy. If it is questionable, we should avoid it.

We should seek to support those we believe will act with integrity and carry out our ideas of good government. The Lord has said: "When the wicked rule the people mourn. Wherefore, honest men and wise men should be sought for diligently, and good men and wise men ye should observe to uphold." (D&C 98:9–10.)

The Church maintains a policy of strict political neutrality, favoring no party or candidate, but every member should take an active part in the political process. We should study the issues and the candidates to be sure our votes are based on knowledge rather than hearsay. We need to pray for our public officials and ask the Lord to help them in making momentous decisions that affect us. Our beliefs regarding earthly governments and laws are summarized in section 134 of the Doctrine and Covenants and the twelfth article of faith. We should support public policy that coincides with these moral beliefs.

Latter-day Saints should seek to carry the gospel message forth to all who will hear it. We should seek without delay to preach by precept and by example, to be sure everyone who is willing to accept the gospel truths has the opportunity to do so. The best way to teach the gospel is to live it. Parents are to prepare their children by teaching them gospel principles, teaching them to live clean, pure lives so they can be worthy missionaries and ambassadors of the Lord, encouraging them to acquire a strong testimony of the gospel, and helping them to prepare financially for this sacred service. Also, older couples should arrange their affairs so they can serve as missionaries.

We can seek to enter holy temples frequently to perform essential ordinances for others who have preceded us. Such work enables us to do for others what they cannot do for themselves, a labor of love that permits our forebears to continue their progress toward eternal life. As valuable as temple work is to them, it is equally valuable to us. The House of the Lord is a place where we can escape from the mundane and see our lives in an eternal perspective. We can ponder instructions and covenants that help us understand more clearly the plan of salvation and the infinite love of our Heavenly Father for his children. We can ponder our relationship to God, the Eternal Father, and his Son, Jesus Christ.

We learn in the Doctrine and Covenants that a temple is a place of thanksgiving, "a place of instruction for all those who are called to the work of the ministry in all their several callings and offices; that they may be perfected in the understanding of their ministry, in theory, in principle, and in doctrine, in all things pertaining to the kingdom of God on the earth." (D&C 97:13–14.) Doing temple work regularly can provide spiritual strength. It can be an anchor in daily life, a source of guidance, protection, security, peace, and revelation. No work is more spiritual than temple work.

In the words of Hugh Nibley, "The temple is a scale model of the universe. The mystique of the temple lies in its extension to other worlds; it is the reflection on earth of the heavenly order, and the power that fills it comes from above."[5] As spirit children of our Heavenly Father, we should seek always to recognize the divine potential within us and never restrict our perspective to the limited scope of mortal life.

We should seek the Holy Ghost, who can be the constant companion of all Latter-day Saints who are obedient and righteous. He can reveal all truth to us in our minds and in our hearts, comfort us in times of distress, prompt us in making correct choices and decisions, and help purify us from sin. I know of no greater blessing that can come to us in mortality than the companionship of the Holy Ghost.

We live in troubled times, but we can seek and obtain the good despite Satan's temptations and snares. He cannot tempt us beyond our power to resist. When we seek "anything virtuous, lovely, or of good report or praiseworthy," we are seeking to emulate the Savior and follow his teachings. Then we are on the path that will lead us to eternal life.

NOTES

1. *History of the Church* 4:535.
2. Richard L. Evans, *Thoughts for One Hundred Days,* vol. 4 (Salt Lake City: Publishers Press, 1970), p. 199.
3. Ezra Taft Benson, "Do Not Despair," *Ensign,* October 1986, p. 2.
4. *HC* 5:134–35.
5. "Nibley Considers the Temple in the Cosmos," *Insights,* March 1992, p. 1.

18

EARNING OUR HERITAGE

Goethe, one of Germany's distinguished poets and philosophers, wrote: "Whatsoever you have inherited from your fathers, you must earn it in order to possess it."

One vital part of the heritage we have received from our fathers that we must earn if we are to possess it is the United States Constitution. Gladstone, a renowned English statesman, said that "it is the most wonderful work ever struck off at a given time by the brain and purpose of man." President Abraham Lincoln admonished us to teach the principles of the Constitution in the schools, in seminaries, and in college. He urged, "Let [it] . . . be written in primers, in spelling books and [wherever possible], let it be preached from the pulpit, proclaimed in legislative halls, and enforced in courts of justice. And, in short, let it become the political religion of the nation."

In a revelation through the Prophet Joseph Smith, the Savior said, "I established the Constitution of this land, by the hands of wise men whom I raised up unto this very purpose." (D&C 101:80.) The Savior established the Constitution so that "every man may act in doctrine and principle pertaining to futurity, according to the moral agency which I have given unto him, that every man may be accountable for his own sins in the day of judgment." (D&C 101:78.)

I believe that we should think seriously about the Constitution and rededicate ourselves to understanding and living by the principles it stands for. As the Savior raised up wise men to establish this tremendous ideal of government, only wise men and women can maintain it. If we do not practice the ideals of the Constitution, we can become anonymous and ineffective.

Our forefathers believed that we should always know what is going on in government and should do our best to keep it relatively small and dedicated to protecting each of us in the enjoyment of life, liberty, and property. We must insist that our government refrain from running our individual lives, so long as we are law-abiding. We must not permit government to take responsibilities that we should bear for ourselves.

More than two hundred years ago, one of the founding fathers of this great nation, Thomas Jefferson, made this observation: "The natural progress of things is for government to gain ground and for liberty to yield." Our obligation as citizens is to help retain the liberty granted to us in the Constitution.

I encourage each of us to think about government, to participate seriously in every phase of it, and to do our part in blocking its tendency to monopolize our lives. If we will do so, we will please the founders of the Constitution. In short, if we earn again what we have inherited, we will never fail.

The story is told that Alexander the Great was puzzled to find Diogenes examining a pile of human bones. "What are you looking for, Diogenes?" asked Alexander. The reply came at once. Said Diogenes, "I am searching for the bones of your father but I cannot distinguish them from his slaves." Life consists of much more than the mere physical, as Diogenes graphically pointed out. The physical alone, as important as it is, makes us individuals of little consequence.

We must become individuals of consequence. We must develop our talents and gifts and become all that we can, making the best possible use of the inheritance given to us by our forefathers. We must learn the truth, love the truth, and live the truth. For, as Abraham Lincoln said so aptly, "The only assurance of our nation's safety is to lay our foundation in morality and religion."

We also must learn to love our progenitors. Vince Lombardi, legendary coach of the Green Bay Packers, told a group of businessmen, "Love is loyalty. Love is teamwork. Love respects the dignity of the individual."[1] To love our forebears and appreciate the heritage we have received from them, we must develop the same great desire that they had for freedom, liberty, and learning.

To make this desire meaningful and practical, we must first relate it to the principles of the gospel. To incorporate gospel principles into our daily lives, we must follow the lives of great men and women in the Church. Their examples are specific and concrete, reducing abstractions to believable, practical principles we can follow.

Think with me of the great inheritances that have been showered upon us, not inheritances of wealth or material things, but of knowledge, faith, and inner strength. These are the spiritual substances that build individuals, productive families, and righteous nations. They are inheritances that we must earn if we are to possess them.

The most important heritage that we can receive is knowledge that the gospel is true. The gospel truths were restored through the Prophet Joseph Smith, under the hands of heavenly beings, by prophets of old and by the Lord himself.

Imagine the glory and intelligence that flowed through the mind of Joseph Smith to the early leaders of the Church as they received the truths of the Godhead, the Atonement, the plan of salvation, the first principles of the gospel, and the organization and mission of the Church. We have the privilege of knowing and loving these truths because our forefathers paid the price of diligence and righteousness and even gave their lives for the upbuilding of the kingdom.

With the restoration of tremendous religious truths came the restoration of the priesthood, the power of God delegated to man on the earth. Most male members of the Church are privileged to bear this holy priesthood. All of our brothers and sisters who are members of the Church enjoy the blessings and power that come from the priesthood of God. With the restoration of the priesthood came the restoration of the saving ordinances of the gospel: baptism, the laying on of hands for the gift of the Holy Ghost, temple endowments, and the sealing of marriage for time and all eternity. What a great privilege is ours to have temples dotting the earth where we can be instructed, blessed, and endowed with power from on high.

We have also inherited the Book of Mormon. If we live according to the principles taught in this inspired record, we will find happiness, strength, and exaltation. It was written for our day and for our problems. It addresses the challenges we face in today's world and will give us additional power to combat the adversary only if we will study and pray to understand its teachings and live by them. President Ezra Taft Benson emphasized again and again how important the reading of the Book of Mormon is to us. When I say "reading," I mean studying and pondering its great truths. He told us many times to read it carefully and prayerfully.

In addition to the Book of Mormon, we have received the Bible, Doctrine and Covenants, and Pearl of Great Price. These sacred scriptures, of divine origin, contain a code for living, born of the commandments of God and the teachings of Jesus Christ. The inspired words of these God-given scriptures constitute a formula for becoming like God and for enjoying a full, happy life.

Our heritage should cause us to focus on our parents. We must not forget them. They have brought us here, given us life, nurtured and taught us, and provided for us throughout our childhood and youth. Most of us have inherited physical and emotional characteristics from our parents. More important, most of us have received from them love, a good example, and teachings of honesty, morality, devotion to what is right, kindness, and respect for others. The crowning blessing of all they have given to us is the restored gospel of Jesus Christ.

For such blessings, we should be eternally grateful. Children brought up in the nurture and admonition of the Lord have the wealth of eternities in their grasp. They see the truths of life as standards of strength, and they grow spiritually toward the ultimate goal of Godhood. Those of us so blessed have inherited a great deal indeed.

Parents generally deserve much more than sons and daughters give back to them by way of tribute or honor. I am grateful to my parents for their careful attention to teaching me to live the principles of honesty in word and deed. My father, for example, was totally honest. He set a great example for the entire family.

One time when I was about seven years old, my father sent me to a hardware store on an errand. He gave me five dollars, which in those days, could buy a great deal. When I arrived home and accounted for my purchases, he counted the change and discovered that the clerk had made a mistake and had given me one dollar too much. The store was about a mile from our home, but he insisted that I walk the entire distance back and return the money.

This was a good lesson. It taught me to always count the change and to make sure I received the correct amount, neither too much nor too little. This is typical of the lessons of honesty he taught us children all during our childhood and teenage years.

How careful are we in our dealings with others? Infractions of the code of honesty are common, but any true Latter-day Saint knows the attitude of the Lord toward such behavior. No man is worthy of his priesthood calling and no woman is without blame who consciously lies, cheats, or steals in any way.

Our task to earn our inheritance in order to possess it is especially important in living a life of sexual purity. A clean heart is part of one's great heritage. Many have received it from their forebears but have not honored it themselves. Others have not received a sacred inheritance of morality but have paid the extra price to repair it and to pass on to their posterity a clean and pure example of virtue, chastity, and modesty.

Satan would have us believe that infractions of the moral code are acceptable because they seem to be so common. "Why worry," he asks, "if you do not control your thoughts or if you allow pornographic or immoral entertainment to be part of your life? Everybody's doing it. It isn't so bad. You can handle it." His logic leads us to rationalize in our minds and suppose that attending just a few R-rated movies or immoral PG-13 movies will not really harm us. And he teaches other to ask, "Are we so unworthy when we watch just two or three questionable programs on the cable television channel? Are the sexually explicit romance novels of the day really so bad?"

These rationalizations, prompted by Satan, become great deterrents to our spiritual growth. Pornography in all of its forms is found at the movies, on television, and in printed form. It constitutes a spiritual poison that is addictive and destructive. Every ounce of pornography and immoral entertainment will drain away a part of our spirituality. Only a little immoral material and entertainment can cause us to lose all of our spiritual strength. The Lord's spirit will not dwell in an unclean tabernacle.

Perhaps Satan would tempt young men and young women further by suggesting that going a little too far in their physical affection with a date is not so serious. After all, they are aware of the main commandments and have no intention of violating them. But what we must remember is that our procreative powers are sacred, beautiful gifts from God and are to be used only in marriage. Sexual activity outside of marriage is forbidden. Physical affection while dating and when a couple are engaged to be married must be limited to the conservative and wholesome and must remain within the bounds the Lord has set. Such expressions of affection are far different from those that are commonly portrayed in the media of our day.

Satan is a master at step-by-step deception. He can make little things seem harmless when, in reality, they quickly bind our spirits and destroy our souls. He makes immodest dress and suggestive behavior seem very acceptable. The ancient prophet Nephi wrote of how Satan deceives us:

"And there shall also be many which shall say: Eat, drink, and be merry; nevertheless, fear God—he will justify in com-

143

mitting a little sin; yea, lie a little, take the advantage of one because of his words, dig a pit for thy neighbor; there is no harm in this; and do all these things, for tomorrow we die; and if it so be that we are guilty, God will beat us with a few stripes, and at last we shall be saved in the kingdom of God.

"Yea, and there shall be many which shall teach after this manner, false and vain and foolish doctrines, and shall be puffed up in their hearts, and shall seek deep to hide their counsels from the Lord; and their works shall be in the dark. . . .

"For the kingdom of the devil must shake, and they which belong to it must needs be stirred up unto repentance, or the devil will grasp them with his everlasting chains, and they be stirred up to anger, and perish; for behold, at that day shall he rage in the hearts of the children of men, and stir them up to anger against that which is good." (2 Nephi 28:8–9, 19–20.)

The desire to acquire spiritual qualities in our lives will lead us to appreciate our inheritance and will help us use this inheritance wisely in every thought and deed. We will receive what we deserve. The Lord has told us: "There is a law, irrevocably decreed in heaven before the foundations of this world, upon which all blessings are predicated—and when we obtain any blessing from God, it is by obedience to that law upon which it is predicated." (D&C 130:20–21.)

We must recognize the hazards of shortcuts and looking for the easy way. We must obey the law and pay the price if we are to receive the reward or achieve the goal.

When James A. Garfield, once president of the United States, was the president of Hiram College, a father brought his son for admittance as a student. The father wanted the boy to take a course shorter than the one offered and exclaimed: "He can never take all that in! He wants to get through quicker. Can you arrange it for him?"

"Oh, yes," replied President Garfield. "He can take a shorter course. It all depends on what you want to make of him. When God wants to make an oak, he takes one hundred years, but he only takes two months to make a squash."[2]

Please remember that we must earn whatever we have inherited from our forebears in order to possess it. This great principle teaches us the formula for developing gratitude, personal strength, service to others, and a genuine testimony of the Lord Jesus Christ.

I would like to add one more ingredient of life that is so important for each of us as individuals, and that is the power of prayer. Prayer has been the great undergirding strength of my life. On many occasions the Lord has answered my prayers, and I bear testimony that nothing brings us more strength and more peace and more answers to today's vexing problems than to speak with the Lord humbly in sacred prayer.

May I relate one experience I had on March 17, 1986. I boarded a plane in Leeds, England, after having conducted a stake conference in that city. The plane I boarded had often been referred to as "the goose." It was given this name because it was so awkward looking. Little did I realize that it was not always reliable mechanically.

We took off in a rainstorm and had been in the air for about fifteen minutes at an altitude of 18,000 feet when the right motor exploded. We lost altitude rapidly. I thought at first that those could be the last moments of my earthly life.

I sat on the second row near the front of the plane, and the cockpit door was open. Observing the anxious and frightened look on the faces of the pilot and co-pilot did not help my anxiety.

The pilot turned the plane around and headed back

toward the Leeds airport. When we're in danger, memories of mistakes we have made in our lives often flash through our minds. This happened to me. The next thought that came to me was to ask for divine intervention from the Lord through fervent prayer. After I had offered my humble prayer, I had a peaceful and calm feeling that we would land safely and all would be well.

As the runway came into our view, it appeared that we would not make it. But suddenly the plane seemed to gain new power, and we landed exactly at the end of the runway. Numerous fire engines and ambulances were standing by, ready to assist if needed. All the passengers breathed a sigh of relief and clapped their hands. Instead of joining with them, I said another silent prayer of thanksgiving for the Lord's intervention.

This was another miracle that occurred in my life, that the Lord is ready and willing to assist when we ask for his help and guidance. May we never forget that prayer in our lives is a necessity—not only in times of danger, but on a day-by-day basis. It will bring us joy and happiness and peace of mind.

NOTES

1. *U. S. News and World Report,* December 5, 1986, p. 153.
2. *Quote Magazine,* January 15, 1987, p. 3.

19

RUNNING OUR MARATHON

In recent years, running has become a popular form of exercise throughout the world. Many run primarily for the exercise, but others run to condition themselves for well-publicized races of various distances. Perhaps the premier endurance race is the marathon, a modern-day race that has its roots in ancient Greece. Today, the meaning of the word *marathon* has been broadened to include any contest or activity of great length that requires extraordinary effort and endurance.

A young friend of mine, whom I will call Alan, recently ran his first marathon—a distance of 26.2 miles. He had set his goal several months in advance, learned what preparation was required, and disciplined himself to follow a rigorous training schedule. He sought the advice of experienced runners and read articles on running a marathon. He practiced running the marathon route and planned a strategy for traversing the hilly course.

Finally, the day of the marathon arrived; it would be the culmination of months of training, discipline, and sacrifice. He got off to a good start in a large crowd of runners. He felt strong and confident, following his predetermined strategy. About eight miles into the race, on a downhill part of the course, he caught up with an experienced runner named

Brent, who had given him sound advice during his training. Alan decided to match his stride to Brent's disciplined and experienced pace.

As they passed the eighteen-mile mark, Alan struggled to stay with Brent so that someone he knew would be by his side if he began "hitting the wall." Hitting the wall means feeling a sudden urge to quit, encountering an almost tangible barrier that requires a tremendous effort to overcome. It often comes at about the twenty-mile mark.

For the next two miles, Alan kept pace with Brent. Then it hit him. He felt a sudden loss of energy, an almost overwhelming desire to stop or walk. "Stay with me," Brent said. "We all feel it at some point. You can get through it. I'll help pull you through."

Somehow Alan continued. He and Brent began to pass spectators. He knew his wife, children, and other family members would be watching about one mile ahead. Drawing on the strength provided by thoughts of his family, he was able to hang on until the desire to quit left him.

As Alan and Brent finally neared the finish, Alan found the last mile to be the hardest of all. The two runners crossed the finish line just five seconds apart. Alan was more exhausted than he ever had been but elated because he had beaten his goal by more than fifteen minutes and had finished among the top twenty-five runners.

In some respects, progressing through life is like running a marathon. Young people are near the beginning of their earthly sojourn. They chose to come to this earth and to be tested and proved, and the end may seem too far away to concern them now. But life, like a marathon, requires a good start and a strong, consistent effort all of the way to the finish.

Just as marathon runners set explicit goals, so should each

of us, young and old alike, look ahead and decide what we want to do with our lives. Now is the time for us to fix clearly in our minds what we want to be or what we want to be doing one year from now, five years, ten years, and beyond. If we have not already received a patriarchal blessing, we should set a goal to receive one and strive to live worthy of its promises. A patriarchal blessing is one of the most important guides in life that members of the Church enjoy. We should write down our goals and review them regularly, keep our goals before us constantly, record our progress, and revise our goals as circumstances dictate. Our ultimate goal should be eternal life—the kind of life God lives, the greatest of all the gifts of God.

After we visualize ourselves as we would like to be in five, ten, or twenty years from now, we should identify the preparation we will need and determine to pay the price in effort, money, study, and prayer. We should be sure we understand the course or path we will be taking. The ideal course of life is not always easy, and comparatively few will find it and complete it. It is not a well-marked freeway, but a narrow path with only one entrance. The way to eternal life is straight and narrow.

When I think of staying on the right path, I am reminded of Lehi's dream about the tree of life. In it, the love of God was likened to a tree that bore delicious fruit that was desirable above all others. Nephi recorded his father's words: "And I also beheld a strait and narrow path, which came along by the rod of iron, even to the tree. . . . And I saw numberless concourses of people, many of whom were pressing forward, that they might obtain the path which led unto the tree." (1 Nephi 8:20–21.) Many of these people later "fell away into forbidden paths and were lost" (v. 28), but those who ignored the scoffing and ridicule of the world and held tightly to the rod of iron enjoyed the fruit of the tree. The rod of iron represents the word of God, which leads us to the love of God. (See 1 Nephi 11:25.) We must hold firmly to the rod of iron through the mists and darkness, the hardships and trials of life. If we relax our grip and slip from the path, the iron rod might become lost in the darkness for a time until we repent and regain our grasp of it.

Remember that success results when preparation meets opportunity in our lives. We will not always know precisely what opportunities will come or when they will come, but we can be sure they will be valuable only to the extent that we are prepared to respond to them. We can see the equation of preparation plus opportunity equaling success in the lives of leaders in the Church, government, business, professions, and, hopefully, in our own lives.

Preparation is vitally important in the Church so that we can do our part when called upon and so that the Lord can use us when he needs us.

In life, as in a marathon, we should seek the help we need, and not depend on our own strength alone. We have never done all we can to finish a task until we have sought help from the Lord, loved ones, Church leaders, and friends.

Relying only on our own abilities can lead to the sin of pride. In the opening section of the Doctrine and Covenants, the Lord described the wicked condition of many in the world: "They seek not the Lord to establish his righteousness, but every man walketh in his own way, and after the image of his own god." (D&C 1:16.) If we boast in our own strength and "walk in our own way," we can slip easily from the straight and narrow path to the broad roadways of the world. We must not be misled by the occasional easiness of the way, like the downhill part of a marathon. Rather, we should keep close to the Lord and trust in him during the easier times, just as we do in our uphill struggles.

Marathon runners pass aid stations located along the course where they receive water, encouragement, and assistance. Without this help, many runners could not carry on. Each of us also have "aid stations" to help us keep moving along our course. These include our parents, other family members, ward leaders, and teachers who have "run more races" and are farther along the path of life. It is important that we benefit from the experience they have accumulated; trust them; seek their advice, counsel, and support; and then listen to them. They will help us stay on course.

We should always be willing, even anxious, to help others. Nothing else we do will give us the same satisfaction and joy within because, we are told, "when ye are in the service of your fellow beings ye are only in the service of your God." (Mosiah 2:17.) Ignoring the needs of others is a serious sin. Alma asked the people of the Church in Zarahemla, "Will ye . . . persist in the wearing of costly apparel and setting your hearts upon the vain things of the world, upon your riches? Yea, will ye persist in supposing that ye are better one than another . . . ? Yea, and will you persist in turning your backs upon the poor, and the needy, and in withholding your substance from them?" (Alma 5:53–55.)

King Benjamin taught that we must care for those in need—the poor, hungry, naked, and sick—both spiritually and temporally if we are to receive a remission of our sins from day to day or, in other words, if we are to walk guiltless before God. (See Mosiah 18:29.)

I suppose that some of us, at one time or another, feel that we are "hitting the wall," which gives us an almost compelling urge to quit, give up, or give in to temptation. Each of us may meet challenges, adversities, and temptations that seem to be more than we can bear. In times of sickness, death, financial need, and other hardships, we may wonder whether we have the strength, courage, or ability to continue.

People today face the same temptations that have been common throughout history, plus many others that were unknown to earlier generations. However, God will not allow us to be tempted beyond our ability to resist. (See 1 Corinthians 10:13.) He does not give us challenges that we cannot surmount. He will not ask more than we can do, but may ask right up to our limits so we can prove ourselves. The Lord will never forsake or abandon anyone. We may abandon him, but he will not abandon us. We never need to feel that we are alone.

The reason to stay on course in a marathon is obvious. Staying on a course that leads to a righteous life may be less obvious but is much more important. In simple terms, a righteous life is the way—the only way—to happiness, joy and peace. We read in the Book of Mormon: "Men are, that they might have joy." (2 Nephi 2:25.)

Our Heavenly Father knows the way for us to enjoy happiness and peace; the principles of the gospel mark the way. They are a gift to us, his children.

The Lord has given us the gift of agency (see Moses 7:32) and instructed us sufficiently to know good from evil (see 2 Nephi 2:5). We are free to choose (see 2 Nephi 2:27) and are permitted to act (see 2 Nephi 10:23; Helaman 14:30), but we are not free to choose the consequences. With absolute certainty, choices of good and right lead to happiness and peace, while choices of sin and evil eventually lead to unhappiness, sorrow, and misery.

An obvious parallel between life and a marathon is the necessity to run diligently and endure to the end. Among Nephi's final words to his people were these: "And now, . . . after ye have gotten into this strait and narrow path, I would ask if all is done? Behold, I say unto you, Nay; . . . Ye must press forward with a steadfastness in Christ . . . and endure to the end." (2 Nephi 31:19–20.) I think of this promise of the Lord: "They that wait upon the Lord shall renew their strength; they shall mount up with wings as eagles; they shall run, and not be weary; and they shall walk, and not faint." (Isaiah 40:31.) We have that promise.

I pray that the Lord will guide each of us in running our personal marathon. Then we can say, as Paul wrote to Timothy, "I have fought a good fight, I have finished my course, I have kept the faith." (2 Timothy 4:7.)

20

Never Give Up

Perseverance means to continue in a given course until we have reached a goal or objective, regardless of obstacles, opposition, and other counter-influences. What is our course, what is our goal, and what are the obstacles and opposition that would hinder or divert us?

Our course as members of the Church of Jesus Christ should be compliance with the principles and ordinances of the gospel. Our goal should be to fill the measure of our creation as sons and daughters of our Heavenly Father—that is, to reach exaltation and eternal life. The obstacles and opposition we meet are the temptations and enticements of Satan designed to frustrate the Lord's work and glory: "To bring to pass the immortality and eternal life of man." (Moses 1:39.)

Perseverance is a positive, active characteristic. It does not mean to idly, passively wait and hope for some good thing to happen. It gives us hope by helping us realize that the righteous suffer no failure except in giving up and no longer trying.

When some people have a difficult job to do, they give up everything else until that job is finished. Others just give up. The need to persevere is expressed in the following lines:

"Genius is only the power of making continuous efforts. The line between failure and success is so fine that we scarcely know when we pass it; so fine that we are often on the line

154

and do not know it. How many a man has thrown up his hands at a time when a little more effort, a little more patience would have achieved success? A little more perseverance, a little more effort, and what seemed a hopeless failure may turn into a glorious success. . . . There is no defeat except within, no really insurmountable barrier save one's own inherent weakness of purpose."[1]

We have numerous examples of perseverance in the scriptures, in secular history, and in our own experiences.

Perhaps the best-known Old Testament example of perseverance is the story of Job. As you know, it narrates the afflictions that befell a righteous man and considers reasons for those afflictions. It does not entirely answer the question of why Job, or anyone, might suffer pain and sorrow, but it does state clearly that affliction is not necessarily a sign of God's anger and a punishment of sin, as Job's friends told him. The book suggests that affliction, if not for punishment, may be for experience, discipline, and instruction.[2]

I do not know of anything that members of the Church need more than they need the conviction and perseverance of Job. He was a just man who feared God and avoided evil. After the Lord allowed Satan to torment Job, Job's afflictions included the loss of his seven sons and three daughters, the loss of his wealth in flocks and herds, and serious physical illnesses. But he remained faithful to the Lord through his indescribable sorrow and suffering, and was able to say, "Blessed be the name of the Lord." (Job 1:21.) "Though he slay me, yet will I trust in him," he declared. ". . . He also shall be my salvation. . . . For I know that my redeemer liveth, and that he shall stand at the latter day upon the earth . . . yet in my flesh shall I see God." (Job 13:15–16; 19:25–26.)

The result of Job's perseverance is told in the conclusion

155

of the story. The Lord blessed him with a family, good health, and great possessions. Job continued in his course, despite unrelenting opposition, until he saw the Lord. (See Job 42:5.)

The Book of Mormon is filled with stories of great people who endured to the very end, from Lehi and his family through Moroni, the son of Mormon. The life of Moroni is especially instructive in teaching perseverance. The obstacles he faced may seem beyond belief to us. He saw the entire Nephite nation destroyed by the sword in a terrible war because of the wickedness of the people. His father and all of his kinsfolk and friends were slain. He was alone for about twenty years, perhaps hiding and fleeing from savage Lamanites who sought to take his life. (See Mormon 8:2–7.) Yet he continued to keep the record as his father had commanded him.

As a result of his perseverance and righteousness, Moroni was ministered to by the Three Nephites, whom the Savior permitted to tarry until his second coming. (See Mormon 8:11.) In these latter days, Moroni had the divine commission of instructing Joseph Smith in his calling as the Prophet of the Restoration and delivering the Book of Mormon record to him.

Joseph Smith's determination and perseverance are other good examples. After reading James 1:5—"If any of you lack wisdom, let him ask of God, that giveth to all men liberally, and upbraideth not; and it shall be given him"—Joseph knew that he must do as James directed or remain in darkness and confusion.

From the moment Joseph knelt in prayer, he encountered enormous obstacles and opposition. First, an evil, unseen power seized him. Then, he wrote, "just at this moment of great alarm, I saw a pillar of light exactly over my head, above the brightness of the sun. . . . It no sooner appeared than I found myself delivered from the enemy which held me bound. When the light rested upon me I saw two Personages, whose brightness and glory defy all description, standing above me. . . . One of them spake unto me, calling me by name and said, pointing to the other—*This is My Beloved Son. Hear Him!*'" (Joseph Smith–History 1:16–17.)

This marvelous event, near the start of the Prophet's mortal ministry, proved to be a pattern in his life. He suffered ridicule, violent attacks by his enemies, betrayal by close associates whom he had trusted, forcible separation from his loved ones, trial and imprisonment on false charges, and, finally, martyrdom at the hands of a mob. Yet he remained true to the charge he had received and served faithfully in his calling as the prophet to usher in the dispensation of the fulness of times. In addition to seeing our Heavenly Father and Jesus Christ, he received instruction and counsel from angels and other heavenly beings throughout his life.

Secular history also teaches the principle of perseverance. Winston Churchill is well known for his determination as a leader of Great Britain during World War II. On one occasion in his later years, he returned to a school where he had studied as a boy. Before he arrived, the headmaster told the students, "The greatest Britisher of our time is going to come to this school, and I want . . . every one of you to be here with your notebooks. I want you to [write] down what he says, because his speech will be something for you to remember all your lives." The elderly statesman came in and was introduced. His glasses were down on the end of his nose, as usual. Then he stood and delivered the following words from an immortal speech that he once gave in Parliament: "Never, never, never give up."[3] And he sat down. That was the speech. It was unmatched.

His message was indeed something to be remembered by every boy who heard it and by each of us. We must never give up, regardless of temptations, frustrations, disappointments, or discouragements.

I believe that perseverance is vital to success in any endeavor, whether spiritual or temporal, large or small, public or personal. Think seriously of how important perseverance, or the lack of it, has been in your own endeavors, such as Church callings, schooling, or employment. I believe that essentially all significant achievement results largely from perseverance.

Through the application of this principle, some of our finest legacies have been produced. For example, John Milton was blind when he wrote *Paradise Lost.* Ludwig von Beethoven was deaf when he finished some of his greatest musical compositions. Abraham Lincoln was laughed at as a gangling, awkward country boy who had many failures, but he became one of the greatest and most eloquent presidents of the United States. Florence Nightingale devoted her life to saving the lives of countless wounded soldiers.

Each of these people left a permanent mark on the world. Their example should give hope to us. They succeeded not only because the Lord had endowed them with gifts, as he has each of us in varying degrees, but also because they applied themselves steadfastly.

Of course, the ultimate example of perseverance is our Lord and Savior, Jesus Christ, who has overcome every obstacle in doing the will of our Heavenly Father. Indeed, Jesus is perfect in perseverance and has taught us to be perfect even as he and his Father are perfect. (See 3 Nephi 12:48.) Studying his life can help us learn and live this important principle.

From the time of the premortal council in which Jesus became the Christ, the Messiah, the Savior of all mankind, through his millennial reign, he persevered in perfection, doing all that his Father commanded. Because of his love for us, he offered to fulfill the plan of salvation with these words: "Father, thy will be done, and the glory be thine forever." (Moses 4:2.) How different this was from Satan's response to the plan: "I will redeem all mankind, that one soul shall not be lost, and surely I will do it; . . . give me thine honor." (Moses 4:1.) The conflict between the forces of evil persists in the world today—with Jesus persevering in striving to save souls, and Satan striving to destroy them.

Through his atonement and resurrection, Jesus provided for all mankind both immortality and the possibility of eternal life. He paid the penalty for our sins if we will repent of them. How grateful I am for the effect upon me of his love and his perseverance!

Probably few of us will face opposition and obstacles like those encountered by the great ones I have mentioned. However, we each have our own challenges and trials to overcome as we strive to keep on the right course. Often the most important trials are those we must face and subdue privately within our own hearts.

I bear testimony that perseverance is essential to us in learning and living the principles of the gospel, and that it will determine our progress as we strive to reach exaltation.

NOTES

1. Author unknown, *Second Encyclopedia,* ed. Jacob M. Brand (Englewood Cliffs, New Jersey: Prentice Hall, 1957), p. 152.
2. See Bible Dictionary, LDS edition of the King James Version, s.v. "Job, Book of."
3. See "These Are Great Days," *War Speeches,* ed. Charles Eada (Boston: Little, Brown and Co., 1942), pp. 286–88.

21

THE IRON ROD

After Lehi left Jerusalem and took his family into the wilderness, he dreamed a dream. He described what he saw in the following verses from the Book of Mormon:

"I saw in my dream, a dark and dreary wilderness. And it came to pass that I saw a man, and he was dressed in a white robe; and he came and stood before me. And it came to pass that he spake unto me, and bade me follow him. And it came to pass that as I followed him I beheld myself that I was in a dark and dreary waste.

"And after I had traveled for the space of many hours in darkness, I began to pray unto the Lord that he would have mercy on me, according to the multitude of his tender mercies. And it came to pass after I had prayed unto the Lord I beheld a large and spacious field. And it came to pass that I beheld a tree, whose fruit was desirable to make one happy. And it came to pass that I did go forth and partake of the fruit thereof; and I beheld that it was most sweet, above all that I ever before tasted. Yea, and I beheld that the fruit thereof was white, to exceed all the whiteness that I had ever seen.

"And as I partook of the fruit thereof it filled my soul with exceedingly great joy; wherefore, I began to be desirous that my family should partake of it also; for I knew that it was desirable above all other fruit.

The Iron Rod

"And as I cast my eyes round about, that perhaps I might discover my family also, I beheld a river of water; and it ran along, and it was near the tree of which I was partaking the fruit. And I looked to behold from whence it came; and I saw the head thereof a little way off; and at the head thereof I beheld your mother Sariah, and Sam, and Nephi; and they stood as if they knew not whither they should go.

"And it came to pass that I beckoned unto them; and I also did say unto them with a loud voice that they should come unto me, and partake of the fruit, which was desirable above all other fruit. And it came to pass that they did come unto me and partake of the fruit also.

"And it came to pass that I was desirous that Laman and Lemuel should come and partake of the fruit also; wherefore, I cast mine eyes towards the head of the river, that perhaps I might see them. And it came to pass that I saw them, but they would not come unto me and partake of the fruit.

"And I beheld a rod of iron, and it extended along the bank of the river, and led to the tree by which I stood. And I also beheld a strait and narrow path, which came along by the rod of iron, even to the tree by which I stood; and it also led by the head of the fountain, unto a large and spacious field, as if it had been a world.

"And I saw numberless concourses of people, many of whom were pressing forward, that they might obtain the path which led unto the tree by which I stood. And it came to pass that they did come forth, and commence in the path which led to the tree.

"And it came to pass that there arose a mist of darkness; yea, even an exceedingly great mist of darkness, insomuch that they who had commenced in the path did lose their way, that they wandered off and were lost.

"And it came to pass that I beheld others pressing forward, and they came forth and caught hold of the end of the rod of iron; and they did press forward through the mist of darkness, clinging to the rod of iron, even until they did come forth and partake of the fruit of the tree." (1 Nephi 8:4–24.)

In the interpretation that Nephi gave, the "rod of iron" meant "the word of God." We must hold fast to it. If we do, we shall never perish, for "neither could the temptations and the fiery darts of the adversary overpower them unto blindness, to lead them away to destruction." (1 Nephi 15:24.)

The world has always been filled with temptations. God's plan was that there be opposition in all things. However, his plan also included the path and the directions that would lead us back to him. If we would stay on the pathway and follow the directions, we must pray always, read the scriptures, keep the commandments, and endure to the end.

1. *Pray always.*

It is significant to note what an important part prayer plays in finding the iron rod. When Lehi saw the man who bid him to follow, he was first led into a dark and dreary waste, where he remained in darkness for many hours until he began to pray to the Lord for his tender mercies. Then he saw the whole picture of his vision. He was led to the tree and was able to partake of the sweet fruit, which was sweeter above all he had ever tasted.

President David O. McKay wrote: "Prayer is the pulsation of a yearning, loving heart in tune with the Infinite. It is a message of the soul sent directly to a loving Father. . . . You cannot imagine an effective prayer without visualizing and feeling a personal God."[1] As we feast upon the word of God, we must talk with the Author of these scriptures to gain understanding and enlightenment.

When we are not in the act of praying, the Lord asks that we have a prayer in our hearts. (See Alma 34:27.) If we are praying to him who is our Creator and asking for guidance and understanding, is not our grasp upon the iron rod? We let go when we stop praying.

We are commanded to pray (Alma 34:17–27) both vocally and in secret. Secret prayer is a personal, private communication that God has provided between us. Elder Francis M. Gibbons wrote: "Satan and his followers, who have been cast out of God's presence and are dead to His spirit, are excluded from those who, by the spirit of prophecy and revelation, may know the thoughts and the intents of our hearts. So, in his wisdom and mercy, God has provided a channel of communication between him and his children on earth that Satan, our common enemy, cannot invade. This is the channel of secret prayer. The significance of this to the Latter-day Saint is profound, for by this means we are able to communicate with our Heavenly Father in secrecy, confident that the adversary cannot intrude."[2]

As parents, if we teach the importance of prayer in our homes, we must pray ourselves. We must have our family prayers morning and night, a blessing on the food at each meal, as well as our personal, private prayers.

We must express to our Heavenly Father our gratitude for all things. The brother of Jared was chastised for failing to call upon the Lord. We are reminded often by our Church leaders to counsel with the Lord, express our gratitude, and ask for those things we stand in need of. We are to pray that our afflictions will be consecrated for our gain. (See 2 Nephi 2:2.) Though at times our memories of this important principle dim, our accountability still remains.

Sincere praying implies that when we ask for any virtue

or blessing, we should work for the blessing and cultivate the virtue. President David O. McKay wrote: "The principle of humility and prayer leads one to feel a need for divine guidance. Self-reliance is a virtue, but with it should go a consciousness of the need of superior help—a consciousness that as you walk firmly in the pathway of duty, there is a possibility of your making a misstep, and with that consciousness is a prayer, a pleading that God will inspire you to avoid that false step."[3]

2. *Reading the scriptures.*

The word of God is all around us. We have his precious word in the scriptures. The Lord has told us the plain and precious truths that will lead us back to him. He has commanded us to read them, to feast upon the word. We must feast upon his word in order to understand our responsibilities. We can't just nibble.

Elder J. Richard Clarke has written, "The holy scriptures are the word of God. If we are to know God, we must read His words, for therein He stands revealed to the honest heart."[4]

It is important to understand that in order to be practicing Latter-day Saints, we must study the scriptures. As Saints, we need to become acquainted with the great heroes of sacred literature and to pattern our lives after them. We don't need to be natural students to read the scriptures; we just need to love the Lord and desire to believe on his word.

A reality of the scriptures is that we never really read them enough. Each time we read the scriptures, we receive new insight, new direction, new information, new strength, a new level of spirituality, and new beauty.

Since feasting on the word of God has a "more powerful effect upon the minds of the people than . . . anything else" (Alma 31:5), the more of the word of God we have and act upon, the more we will press forward. Much spiritual energy is necessary for the marathon of discipleship. As Elder Neal A. Maxwell has said, "If we fail to attend the feast, if we do not search the scriptures, we will miss the needed and reminding truths that God has sent among us for that purpose."[5]

President Marion G. Romney declared: "I don't know much about the gospel other than what I've learned from the standard works. When I drink from a spring I like to get the water where it comes out of the ground, not down stream after the cattle have waded in it. . . . I appreciate other people's interpretation, but when it comes to the gospel we ought to be acquainted with what the Lord says . . . You ought to read the Book of Mormon and the Doctrine and Covenants; and . . . all the scriptures with the idea of finding out what's in them and what the meaning is and not to prove some idea of your own. Just read them and plead with the Lord to let you understand what he had in mind when he wrote them."[6]

The motto of Bible week in 1989 was: "To Know Where You're Going, Read the Bible." That is the purpose of the scriptures: to give us direction, to be a road map for life, to keep us holding to the iron rod.

In the scriptures we find information expressed so simply that any mind can in some degree grasp it, yet so sublime and so great that when we come to investigate its depths, it requires greater powers and greater understanding than what man naturally possesses.

We are admonished to "search the scriptures; for they are they which testify" of the Savior. (John 5:39.)

We are so fortunate to have the fullness of the gospel with additional scriptures that give us added understanding and direction. Without access to a fullness of scriptures, people substitute deliberation for revelation. It is the truth that makes us free. (John 8:32.)

As long as man continues to dwell outside God's presence, the search for his word and the meaning of his word must continue. It is still a major access to him. The Prophet Joseph Smith taught:

"Search the scriptures—search the revelations which are published and ask your Heavenly Father, in the name of His Son Jesus Christ, to manifest the truth unto you, and if you do it with an eye single to His glory nothing doubting, He will answer you by the power of His Holy Spirit. You will then know for yourselves and not for another. You will not then be dependent on man for the knowledge of God; nor will there by any room for speculation. . . . For when men receive their instruction from Him that made them, they know how He will save them. . . . Again we say: Search the Scriptures, search the Prophets and learn what portion of them belongs to you."[7]

3. *Keep the commandments.*

Holding to the iron rod requires that we keep the commandments. Learning the gospel from the written word is not enough. It must also be lived.

President Spencer W. Kimball counseled us to "hold fast to the iron rod. The Savior urged us to put our hand to the plow without looking back. In that spirit we are being asked to have humility and a deep and abiding faith in the Lord and to move forward—trusting in him, refusing to be diverted from our course, either by the *ways* of the world or the *praise* of the world. I see that quality of readiness and devotion in our people today. There is so much yet to be done! Let us, then, move forward; let us continue the journey with lengthened stride. The Lord will lead us along, and he will be in our midst and not forsake us."[8]

Jesus said, "If ye love me, keep my commandments." (John 14:15.) We bring glory to our Creator by keeping his law and setting a good example as his disciples. True happiness in this life and the life to come is found in keeping the commandments of God. We should "live by every word that proceedeth forth from the mouth of God." (D&C 84:44.)

The Ten Commandments focus on our relationships with God, self, parents, and neighbors. Further commandments add detail. In addition to honoring God, we are to honor our parents. We are to honor others. We are to esteem neighbors as ourselves. We honor God by surrendering to God, by giving away our sins—by putting at his feet the old self, old baggage, old equipment, and so on. Doing this ensures our getting to know God, and it brings greater richness in other relationships too.

Elder Neal A. Maxwell explains, "What seems so plain— keeping the commandments in one's daily life—is 'it!' There is not something else of a higher order which we are supposed to be doing instead."[9] This is truly exercising free agency. We are actually free to make choices.

King Benjamin reminds us of the blessed and happy state of those who keep the commandments of God. They will "dwell with God in a state of never-ending happiness. O remember, remember that these things are true; for the Lord God hath spoken it." (Mosiah 2:41.)

4. *Endure to the end.*

Nephi admonishes us: "And now, my beloved brethren, after ye have gotten into this strait and narrow path, I would ask if all is done? Behold, I say unto you, Nay; for ye have not come thus far save it were by the word of Christ with unshaken faith in him, relying wholly upon the merits of him who is mighty to save.

"Wherefore, ye must press forward with a steadfastness in Christ, having a perfect brightness of hope, and a love of God and of all men. Wherefore, if ye shall press forward, feasting upon the word of Christ, and endure to the end, behold, thus saith the Father: Ye shall have eternal life." (2 Nephi 31:19–20.)

It is vital for us to realize that life's real difficulties are "but for a small moment" and to trust in God's timetable.

Elder Maxwell has written: "Enduring brings such a rich supply of experience, of opportunities to use our moral agency, especially when we take Jesus' yoke upon us in order to learn of Him in an accelerated way: 'Take my yoke upon you, and learn of me; for I am meek and lowly in heart; and ye shall find rest unto your souls' (Matthew 11:29). Experience, however, cannot be rushed. Experience requires time. And time requires patience."[10]

We came to this earth to experience resistance. It was part of the plan. The law of opposition makes freedom of choice possible. The Lord told Joseph Smith: "Thine adversity and thine afflictions shall be but a small moment; and then, if thou endure it well, God shall exalt thee on high. . . . If thou art called to pass through tribulation, . . . know thou, my son, that all these things shall give thee experience, and shall be for thy good." (D&C 121:7–8; 122:5, 7.)

"Being human, we would expel from our lives physical pain and mental anguish and assure ourselves of continual ease and comfort," President Kimball taught, "but if we were to close the doors upon sorrow and distress, we might be excluding our greatest friends and benefactors. Suffering can make saints of people as they learn patience, long-suffering, and self-mastery."[11]

The word of God is sweeter than all others. We must hold onto these precious things so that we will not be led into temptations and overcome by the adversary. The word gives us understanding of our purpose and direction in life. May we be loyal and true in our faith, in saying our prayers, in keeping the commandments, and in enduring to the end.

Notes

1. David O. McKay, *Treasures of Life,* comp. Clare Middlemiss (Salt Lake City: Deseret Book, 1963), p. 308.
2. Francis M. Gibbons, "The Dual Aspects of Prayer," *Ensign,* November 1991, p. 78.
3. McKay, *Treasures of Life,* p. 311.
4. J. Richard Clarke, "My Soul Delighteth in the Scriptures," *Ensign,* November 1982, p. 15.
5. Neal A. Maxwell, *A Wonderful Flood of Light* (Salt Lake City: Bookcraft, 1990), p. 53.
6. Marion G. Romney, address delivered at coordinators' convention, Seminaries and Institutes of Religion, April 13, 1973.
7. *Teachings of the Prophet Joseph Smith,* pp. 11–12.
8. Spencer W. Kimball, "Let Us Not Weary in Well Doing," *Ensign,* May 1980, p. 81.
9. Maxwell, *A Wonderful Flood of Light,* p. 103.
10. Ibid., p. 90.
11. Spencer W. Kimball, *Faith Precedes the Miracle* (Salt Lake City: Deseret Book Co., 1972), p. 98.

22

THE WILL OF THE LORD

In our minds, let's go back to the meridian of time and be with the Savior as he teaches the multitude: "But when ye pray, use not vain repetitions, as the heathen do: for they think that they shall be heard for their much speaking. Be not ye therefore like unto them: for your Father knoweth what things ye have need of, before ye ask him. After this manner therefore pray ye: Our Father which art in heaven, hallowed be thy name. Thy kingdom come. Thy will be done in earth, as it is in heaven." (Matthew 6:7–10.)

The Savior taught that our Father knows what things we have need of before we ask him. And because the Father knows, the Savior teaches us to pray for that *will* to be done on earth as in heaven.

Let us stretch our minds for a moment and contemplate the heavens. The Prophet Joseph Smith taught: "Thy mind, O man! . . . must stretch as high as the utmost heavens."[1]

What is heaven? A "heavenly life" is what we seek. When something is wonderful beyond words, we say it is "heavenly." In the world, the word *heaven* refers to something that is ideal and sublime. In heaven, would we be hungry? In heaven, would we feel alone? In heaven, would we be bored or feel unfulfilled? In heaven, would we fight and bicker? In heaven, would we find any of the things that cause us great concern and emptiness on earth? Or would heaven be just heavenly?

It would be the expansion and concentration of all of God's love. The heaven we are referring to here is the heaven where God dwells. Therefore, the heavenly life is God's life, or eternal life; it is the kind of life that God lives.

Does God not have all power and knowledge? Aware then of all options and alternatives if there were a better life to be had in all the expanse of eternity, would he not have that life for himself and for his family? Heavenly life is simply the best life. It is worth any price.

In heaven they do God's will. That is why it is heaven. We so often say "it's God will." What does that really mean to us? Why is that so important, and how can we determine his will? Of course, we cannot really comprehend all of his will. He has told us, "For my thoughts are not your thoughts, neither are your ways my ways, saith the Lord. For as the heavens are higher than the earth, so are my ways higher than your ways, and my thoughts than your thoughts." (Isaiah 55:8–9.) However, we do know some things about the nature of God.

We know to some degree that as we are now, God once was; and as he is, we may become. In other words, he knows this path, having been this way before. He is the manifestation of our potential. We know that it is perfected. He has perfect knowledge, power, and feelings. He loves us with a perfect love. He cares for us with a perfect caring. He desires for us to become like him, to share in all that he has, and to experience the ultimate existence. This knowledge as foundation for faith is essential.

From the Lectures on Faith we learn that the first principle upon which faith rests is the idea that God exists, and that we need correct knowledge about his attributes. We cannot have faith in a being we know nothing about. For example, it is important to know that he is perfect and does not vary from day to day. How could we have faith in a being that is as varied or as moody as we may be?

The next step on the path of pure, whole faith is to know that the life we are living is pleasing to him, and that we are living in harmony with his will. The scriptures tell us: "The world passeth away, and the lust thereof: but he that doeth the will of God abideth for ever" (1 John 2:17); "Nevertheless, he that endureth in faith and doeth my will, the same shall overcome, and shall receive an inheritance upon the earth when the day of transfiguration shall come" (D&C 63:20).

Sometimes as human beings we may feel a little rebellious, and we may want to do things in our own way. At times like this, let us remember the loving and all-knowing nature of our Father in Heaven and his desire for us to become like him. Freedom is the ability to choose between alternatives, and the greatest freedom is the power and ability to choose from all possible alternatives. That is a condition we can gain only as we live the way he wants us to live and become like him.

To understand the desirability of living in harmony with the will of our Father in Heaven, we must learn and understand his will and then do that will. How can we learn his will? The fundamental principle is the principle of revelation—God communicating with man. Past revelation records how the Lord has dealt with some of his children in times past. The scriptures, then, provide case histories of how the Lord has dealt with various people in various situations, and help us to learn more about our Father's will.

This is similar to what happens in a marriage relationship. As we come to understand the actions, wants, and desires of our spouse, we learn more about his or her mind. So it is with the Lord. We cannot understand many of the things he is trying to tell us or has told us unless we know his ways; then we can begin to understand his mind and will.

To many people, reading the scriptures is a task that is bound with feelings of duty rather than excitement. President Brigham Young gave a great key to making the scriptures have greater meaning to us. He said: "Do you read the scriptures, my brethren and sisters, as though you were writing them a thousand, two thousand or five thousand years ago! Do you read them as though you stood in the place of the men who wrote them?"[2] When we do as President Young admonishes us, we open ourselves up to more inspiration and revelation.

In our own lives today, we receive revelation through the still, small voice that whispers "Yes, that applies to me." The Prophet Joseph Smith received this kind of revelation when he read in James 1:5 that he should pray and ask God. It was in a similar circumstance that President Joseph F. Smith, after reading and contemplating the scriptures, had the vision of the redemption of the dead (D&C 138) opened to his mind. Regular study of the scriptures and meditating upon them are essential for continual revelation.

A process of revelation is described by the Lord in the ninth section of the Doctrine and Covenants, when Oliver Cowdery wanted to help the Prophet Joseph Smith in translating the Book of Mormon. Oliver was taught that he must study things out in his mind and approach the Lord in prayer before the Lord would confirm the truth. It is important to understand that such reasonings are usually spiritual reasoning, and to review in our minds what the Lord has already told us or what he has told others in past scripture and revelation.

173

That is the kind of preparation described by Moroni prior to the promise given in Moroni 10:4 for a testimony concerning the Book of Mormon: "Remember how merciful the Lord hath been unto the children of men, from the creation of Adam even down until the time that ye shall receive these things." (Moroni 10:3.)

Prayer is the key as we open our hearts, seek the Lord, and seek to understand. If we ask, it shall be given; knock, and it shall be opened.

In the vocabulary of revelation, it is important to learn, to listen, and to understand as we pray. Remember again the words of the Savior, who said that the Father knows what we have need of before we ask him. When we open our hearts in prayer, we tune in our souls to hear and understand.

If we stop and feel during prayer, we sometimes hear a still small voice, which enters quietly into our mind and heart. It is so simple and so precise that we often pass it by, thinking that it is just our own idea or a passing thought, not revelation. However, as we reconcile these whisperings to what we know to be true, we soon learn to recognize them; and by recognizing them, we become more able to listen carefully.

The voice of the Spirit has a characteristic of being precise, simple, and penetrating. For example, we may pray, "Father, please help me to become a better parent," and the quiet voice says, *Don't yell at your children.* And we say, "Oh, that is just my own thinking—that couldn't be from the Lord."

A young man may pray, "Father in Heaven, please help me to get better grades," and the little voice says, *Get up early and study.* And the young man says, "That couldn't be the voice of the Lord—that's simple and that's too hard. What I really need is the Lord's help in getting good grades on the test."

Or a young woman may pray, "Father in Heaven, help me to know if I should marry Bill," and the quiet voice says, *You know that Bill does not have a strong testimony.* And she says to herself, "Well, yes, but that couldn't be an answer to prayer. That is just my own worry. What I need to know is, Should I marry Bill?"

The answers to prayers often have a familiar spirit, for the Lord has already given us answers through Church policy, the scriptures, or counsel from the General Authorities at general conference. If we would only think first, sometimes we would have less need to ask except to gain confirmation by the Spirit. We don't have to ask the Lord whether we should marry outside of the temple.

One helpful approach to determining the will of the Lord is to try to ask important questions during times when we know we are in tune. We are in tune when we go to a beautiful testimony meeting and feel tears forming in our eyes. We know we are on the right wavelength when we feel the sweetness and love for the gospel as we pray; and as we ask, we feel good, our thoughts are positive, and it seems right. We have received the witness. That doesn't mean the witness will not fade and that there will not be temptations and fears as we approach the day at the altar. But we have had a witness, and now we must live true to the witness.

In contrast, suppose that in that special moment, we ask and then doubts come into our minds. We are full of concern, and the soft assurance doesn't come at that moment. How did we feel during one of our best moments? Maybe we didn't feel very good. Is that not a clear answer, one that now requires our action?

Ofttimes we complain about not knowing the will of the Lord when actually we do know—or at least suspect we know—but we prefer to live with the question rather than the answer. An example of this kind of inner dishonesty would be a person who seeks the Lord's will concerning marriage to a particular mate with whom he or she has a deep emotional or physical attraction but who has not had the question confirmed by the Spirit. Instead of bowing to the Lord's love and wisdom, the person goes ahead with the marriage, preferring to live with the question rather than the answer. Such misjudgment brings dire consequences that must be guarded against continually.

Now, having determined the necessity of attuning our will to that of the Father's, we come to the most challenging part of our gospel life: learning *to do* the will of the Lord. Section three of the Doctrine and Covenants gives us some very important insight on this point: "For although a man may have many revelations, and have power to do many mighty works, yet if he boasts in his own strength, and sets at naught the counsels of God, and follows after the dictates of his own will and carnal desires, he must fall and incur the vengeance of a just God upon him." (D&C 3:4.)

There are so many influences on our will, things of the flesh, things of men, that to conquer our will and to be able to offer to the Lord a broken heart and contrite spirit is a considerable challenge. (See John 1:13.) This is the process of being born again to a new life, a life that is oriented to service and the Savior.

Probably the most profound and instructive experience of conquering one's will and making one's answer be "Thy will be done" is found in the touching scene in the garden as the Savior prayed. He cried out to the Father with his mortal voice, "Father, if it be possible, let this cup pass from me," and then answered with his pure heart: "Nevertheless not as I will, but as thou wilt." (Matthew 26:39.)

Even the perfect life of the Savior was such that when faced with the greatest challenge in the eternities, he prayed that he might not partake. But trusting himself to the Father, he submitted and partook, became fully glorified, and received of the Father's fullness. (See D&C 93.)

Each of us approaches many tasks in life. Whether in the quiet struggles that few see or the more obvious Gethsemanes, we struggle to control ourselves and to submit ourselves. I believe that alone, we cannot be successful. Satan is too clever, the temptations of the world and of ego and of pride are too great, and the test is too long. But through the Mediator, we can succeed. He passed this way before us, and he has paid the price.

This leads us to the process of making covenants and participating in ordinances, which are sources of power as we realize the importance of the Lord's will in our lives and have faith in it. Such faith turns us toward the Savior, his life, and his unconditional love for us. As these truths sink into our hearts, we hear him requiring the sacrifice of a broken heart and contrite spirit. We must give up the ways of the world and accept and do his way.

We need to develop the "do it" approach. Often we go through periods of struggle and concern to determine the will of the Lord, and then, as a great temptation is in our path, we approach it as if we were going to labor and wrestle all the night to overcome the opposition. Yet often all we need to do is to *not* do it when we are being tempted. It is easier to get up in the morning for five minutes of scripture study than to worry and struggle over it for very long. Soon we get to the point at which we forget about all the gimmicks we need to help us, and we just *do it.*

Doing the will of the Lord is the whole essence of the priesthood process: we have authority to do the will of the Lord, not what we please. That is what the priesthood is. The power of the priesthood, coupled with proper authority, brings the full blessings it offers. This is the same process for the sisters and in the ministry of motherhood. The power comes when we take care to do the Lord's will in the details of child rearing.

I bear testimony that our Father does have all knowledge and power. He does love us absolutely and wants for us the best. That is his will. My prayer is that we will listen and *do.*

NOTES

1. *Teachings of the Prophet Joseph Smith,* p. 137.
2. *Journal of Discourses* 7:33.

23

WITHOUT GUILE

Early in his mortal ministry, the Savior soon had a multitude of disciples drawn to him by the power of his presence and the spirit of his message. From among these disciples, he chose twelve to be his special witnesses. "And when it was day, he called unto him his disciples: and of them he chose twelve, whom also he named apostles." (Luke 6:13.)

Clearly, Jesus had chosen these witnesses, for he said, "Ye have not chosen me, but I have chosen you, and ordained you." (John 15:16.) These twelve were common men from various walks of life. The Savior selected them because he could see far beyond their earthly appearance and look into their hearts, recognizing their potential.

After the Savior called Peter, Andrew, and Philip, Philip introduced him to Nathanael, whom some scholars believe to be the apostle Bartholomew. Philip told Nathanael, "We have found him, of whom Moses in the law, and the prophets, did write, Jesus of Nazareth, the son of Joseph" (John 1:45), thus testifying that Jesus is the Messiah. Nathanael wondered whether any good thing could come out of Nazareth, indicating the relatively bad reputation of that community in those days. Philip asked him to come and see. This is the perfect answer to all who seek to know the truth about Christ.

Open-minded investigators may be converted when they come and see.

When Jesus saw Nathanael coming toward him, he exclaimed, "Behold an Israelite indeed, in whom is no guile!" At that moment, Nathanael recognized that Jesus could see into his heart and asked, in surprise, "Whence knowest thou me?" The Savior's reply demonstrated an even greater power of perception. He said that before Philip had called him (Nathanael) to come and see, Jesus had seen him under a fig tree.

Nathanael apparently had undergone some surpassing spiritual experience while praying, meditating, or worshipping under a fig tree. The Lord, though absent in body, had been present with him in spirit. Nathanael then recognized the Savior as the Christ and said, "Rabbi, thou art the Son of God; thou art the King of Israel." (John 1:47–49.)

Nathanael spoke without guile. The words came from his heart. They expressed a deep conviction of truth. He followed the Savior.

To be without guile is to be free of deceit, cunning, hypocrisy, and dishonesty in thought or action. To beguile is to deceive or lead astray, as Lucifer beguiled Eve in the Garden of Eden. A person without guile is a person who is innocent, who has honest intent and pure motives, and whose life reflects the simple practice of conforming daily actions to principles of integrity.

The psalmist wrote, "Blessed is the man unto whom the Lord imputeth not iniquity, and in whose spirit there is no guile" (Psalm 32:2), and then admonished, "Keep thy tongue from evil, and thy lips from speaking guile" (Psalm 34:13).

In the New Testament, we learn that the Savior was without guile (see 1 Peter 2:22) and that "he that will love life, and see good days, let him refrain his tongue from evil, and his lips that they speak no guile" (1 Peter 3:10).

In latter-day scriptures, we read that the Lord called Edward Partridge to be bishop for the Church because of his pure heart, "for he is like unto Nathanael of old, in whom there is no guile." (D&C 41:11.) In another revelation the Lord said, "My servant George Miller is without guile; he may be trusted because of the integrity of his heart; and for the love which he has to my testimony I, the Lord, love him." (D&C 124:20.)

These passages of scripture help me understand what the Lord could see in Nathanael, Edward Partridge, and George Miller, and give me some insight into what he expects of the Saints. I believe the Savior was seeking purity of soul in those he called to be his twelve apostles. When he spoke of being without guile, he referred to something far deeper than outward appearance. He was reaching into the soul, to the very heart of righteousness. He was touching the key to goodness and to the Christlike life.

To be without guile is to be pure in heart, an essential virtue of those who would be counted among true followers of Christ. He taught in the Sermon on the Mount: "Blessed are the pure in heart: for they shall see God." (Matthew 5:8; see also 3 Nephi 12:8.) He revealed to the Prophet Joseph Smith that Zion is the pure in heart (see D&C 97:21), and that a house is to be built in Zion in which the pure in heart shall see God (see D&C 97:10–16).

If we are without guile, we are honest, true, and righteous. These are all attributes of Deity and are required of the Saints. Those who are honest are fair and truthful in their speech, straightforward in their dealings, free of deceit, and above stealing, misrepresentation, or any other fraudulent action.

Honesty is of God; dishonesty of the devil, who was a liar from the beginning. Righteousness means living a life that is in harmony with the laws, principles, and ordinances of the gospel.

As parents know, little children are, by their nature, guileless. They speak the thoughts of their minds without reservation or hesitation. They do not deceive. They set an example of being without guile. The Savior taught about this attribute when his disciples asked, "Who is the greatest in the kingdom of heaven?

"And Jesus called a little child unto him, and set him in the midst of them, and said, Verily I say unto you, Except ye be converted, and become as little children, ye shall not enter into the kingdom of heaven. Whosoever therefore shall humble himself as this little child, the same is greatest in the kingdom of heaven." (Matthew 18:1–4.)

On another occasion, he referred again to the purity of children: "Then were there brought unto him little children, that he should put his hands on them, and pray: and the disciples rebuked them. But Jesus said, Suffer little children, and forbid them not, to come unto me: for of such is the kingdom of heaven." (Matthew 19:13–14.)

To the Nephites, the Savior said, "Ye must repent, and be baptized in my name, and become as a little child, or ye can in nowise inherit the kingdom of God." (3 Nephi 11:38.)

"He commanded that their little children should be brought. So they brought their little children and set them down upon the ground . . . and Jesus stood in the midst; and the multitude gave way till they had all been brought unto him. . . . He took their little children, one by one, and blessed them, and prayed unto the Father for them. . . . And . . . angels did minister unto them." (3 Nephi 17:11–12, 21, 24.)

Without Guile

What a great responsibility rests with parents to be certain that they do nothing to alter or destroy the guileless innocence of their little ones!

I believe that the necessity for Latter-day Saints to be without guile may be more urgent now than at other times because many in the world apparently do not understand the importance of this virtue or are indifferent to it. We see and hear reports of fraud and deception in all levels of our society. A few citizens of some nations betray their country by exchanging sensitive information for money, information they have stolen or with which they have been entrusted. The entertainment industry seems to have lost, in large measure, the concept of moral values. Employees falsify expense accounts. These few examples of guile illustrate how pervasive it is.

Of far greater concern than the outward acts of guile are the inner feelings and the attitudes that motivate them. Fraud and deception appear to be increasingly acceptable; the only wrongdoing seems to be in being caught. The objective often is to get gain or to profit, regardless of the injury, loss, or damage to others. This attitude is totally contrary to the principles of the gospel. It hinders or thwarts the spiritual progress of anyone afflicted by it. The practice of guile prevents the Holy Ghost from prompting, guiding, and instructing us, leaving us ever more susceptible to the buffetings of Satan. When we break the commandments, we close ourselves to God's influence and open ourselves to Satan's influence.

If we practice guile in small matters, we soon find ourselves entangled in an ever-increasing, unending spiral, because each lie or other deception often requires a larger one to cover the first. Moreover, the practice of guile often leads to hypocrisy, which is the false pretense of virtue or righteousness and pretending to be something that we are not. If we know what is right and profess to live by that knowledge but, in fact, do not, we are hypocrites. The Savior denounced hypocrites in unmistakable language. He declared: "Woe unto you, scribes and Pharisees, hypocrites! for ye are like unto whited sepulchres, which indeed appear beautiful outward, but are within full of . . . all uncleanness. Even so ye also outwardly appear righteous unto men, but within ye are full of hypocrisy and iniquity." (Matthew 23:27–28.)

To the Prophet Joseph Smith, the Lord revealed: "Wo unto them that are deceivers and hypocrites, for, thus saith the Lord, I will bring them to judgment. . . . [They] shall be detected and shall be cut off, . . . and wo unto them who are cut off from my church, for the same are overcome of the world." (D&C 50:6, 8.)

What are the Latter-day Saints to do? The answer is plain. We are to be absolutely without guile in every aspect of our lives: in our homes and families, Church callings, business dealings, and especially the private and personal areas of our lives into which only we and the Lord see.

I suggest that we look into our hearts and see whether or not our motives and actions are pure and above reproach and if we are free of deceit and fraud. Perhaps each of us can ask ourself a few questions.

Am I totally free of guile in my conversations and associations with my spouse and my children so that they always know what to expect and always have unquestioning trust and confidence in me?

Am I forthright in my interviews with my bishop and other priesthood leaders?

If I am a student, am I true to myself, my classmates, and

my teachers, even if a little cheating might improve my grades?

If I work for a company or an individual, do I do more work than my employer expects or requires, and am I always alert for ways to do my work better?

If I am an employer, do I pay my employees fairly for their labors?

Do I file accurate tax returns?

Am I scrupulous in all business transactions to the extent that my associates always know they are being treated fairly and would feel secure if they had no contract?

Am I satisfied with my personal standards of integrity, morality, and honesty? Can I say of myself, as Jesus said of Nathanael, that I am without guile?

Some may think that the ideal of a society without guile is preposterous in this day. If so, it is because of the power Satan has over the hearts of many. With the Lord's help, we can be without guile. Being honest and fair helps rather than hinders success and prosperity.

During a visit to the land of Chile, my wife and I visited people who were without guile almost to the point of possessing the naive innocence of little children. We were humbled and refreshed to be among them. They strengthened our faith in mankind and our hope for the future.

Yes, the Saints can be free of guile—and must be, to be prepared for the Savior's second coming. We can provide a leavening influence in the world and can demonstrate the value of living guilelessly. As we develop this divine attribute, we can become a shining light to the world. Certainly, we can teach the principles of the gospel and bless the families of the earth by following the perfect example of the Savior, who is totally without guile.

Visualize in your mind a society in which all are pure in heart and completely free of deceit and dishonesty. Can you imagine a total absence of contention and disputes, with no one ever attempting to deceive another? How would life be if we always were certain, without question, that what others represent to us is true? Theft would be unknown. We would have little use for jails or prisons, and litigation would be rare. The greatest blessing that would come to a society without guile is the personal inner peace that comes to those who know they are doing the right and that their lives are acceptable to the Lord.

A society without guile is possible. I cite two examples from the scriptures. The first is the City of Holiness, even Zion, a city in which the inhabitants were pure in heart and dwelt in righteousness. That city, referred to as the city of Enoch, was taken up into heaven. (See Moses 7:18–21.)

The second example is the society of the Nephites that lasted for about two hundred years after the resurrected Lord visited and taught them. (See 4 Nephi 1.)

Though we know that we must perfect our lives grace upon grace and line upon line (see John 1:16; 2 Nephi 28:30), these are examples of the goal of perfection that we should strive for.

24

Personal Integrity

In a revelation given to the Prophet Joseph Smith, the Lord said, "Blessed is my servant Hyrum Smith; for I, the Lord, love him because of the integrity of his heart, and because he loveth that which is right." (D&C 124:15.) I personally know of no higher praise that any person could receive.

To me, integrity means to always do what is right and good, regardless of the immediate consequences. It means being righteous from the very depths of our soul, not only in our actions but, more importantly, in our thoughts and in our hearts. Personal integrity implies such trustworthiness and incorruptibility that we are incapable of being false to a trust or covenant.

We all have within us the ability to know what is right and good. Speaking to the "peaceable followers of Christ," the prophet Mormon said:

"It is given unto you to judge, that ye may know good from evil; and the way to judge is as plain, that ye may know with a perfect knowledge, as the daylight is from the dark night.

"For behold, the Spirit of Christ is given to every man, that he may know good from evil; wherefore, I show unto you the way to judge; for every thing which inviteth to do good, and to persuade to believe in Christ, is sent forth by the power and gift of Christ; wherefore ye may know with a perfect knowledge it is of God.

"But whatsoever thing persuadeth men to do evil, and believe not in Christ, and deny him, and serve not God, then ye may know with a perfect knowledge it is of the devil; for after this manner doth the devil work, for he persuadeth no man to do good, no, not one; neither do his angels; neither do they who subject themselves unto him." (Moroni 7:3, 15–17.)

Having received the Spirit of Christ to know good from evil, we should always choose the good. We need not be misled, even though fraud, deception, deceit, and duplicity often seem to be acceptable in the world today. Integrity—a firm adherence to the highest moral and ethical standards—is essential to the life of a true Latter-day Saint.

Like Job of old, we need to say, "Till I die I will not remove mine integrity from me." (Job 27:5.) Though Job had lost almost everything he valued—his family, his friends, his health, his wealth—he refused to give up his integrity.

Joseph, the son of Jacob, was a model of integrity. His integrity placed him among the greatest of our Heavenly Father's sons. He did what was right and good. He was trustworthy and incorruptible, self-disciplined, and never violated a trust.

Because of his integrity and righteousness, Joseph was favored and blessed of the Lord in every circumstance. His life is evidence that "all things work together for good to [those who] love God." (Romans 8:28.) His example is especially pertinent to us because most members of the Church have descended from his loins.

Joseph's father, Jacob, loved him even from his youth. The Lord revealed future events to Joseph in dreams. However, his brothers hated him, plotted to take his life, and then sold him as a slave. When he was carried captive to Egypt, the Lord was with him there. Joseph became overseer of the house of Potiphar, captain of Pharaoh's guard. When approach by Potiphar's wife, Joseph refused and fled from her improper advances because of his personal righteousness and because he would not violate Potiphar's trust.

This refusal and the accusations it prompted cause Joseph to be imprisoned. Again the Lord was with him, for he became overseer of the prison. The Lord enabled him to interpret the dreams of Pharaoh's butler and baker; and later, he interpreted Pharaoh's own dreams of seven fat and lean cows and of seven full and thin ears of corn. Subsequently, Joseph became ruler over all Egypt, second in rank only to Pharaoh. He directed the storage of food during the years of plenty and the dispensing of it during the years of famine.

During the famine, Joseph's brothers, who had sold him as a slave twenty-two years earlier, came to Egypt to obtain food. Not recognizing him, they bowed down to him because of his high office. Then, in a tender, touching scene, Joseph identified himself and forgave his brothers. I suppose he could have retaliated for their mistreatment of him by making them slaves, having them imprisoned, or even having them put to death. But he did what was right and good. He said: "I am Joseph your brother, whom ye sold into Egypt. Now therefore be not grieved, nor angry with yourselves, that ye sold me hither. . . . And God sent me before you to preserve you a posterity, . . . and to save your lives by a great deliverance. So now it was not you that sent me hither, but God." (Genesis 45:4–5, 7–8.)

Through Joseph, the Lord preserved the children of Israel

and provided a place in Egypt for them to flourish and increase.

This story is well known, but I urge you to read it again, focusing your attention on the integrity of Joseph and the blessing it brought to him. He became the birthright son in the house of Israel and received an inheritance in the lands of the Americas. (See Ether 13:8.) The Lord permitted him to prophesy of Moses, who would deliver the children of Israel out of Egypt (see JST Genesis 50:27–29), and of Joseph Smith, the prophet of the restoration of the gospel in the latter days (see JST Genesis 50:30–33; 2 Nephi 3:6–21).

Someone has said that "a man's true greatness is not in what he says he is, nor what people say he is; but in what he really is." Our integrity determines what we really are.

Such an example of integrity was George Washington, first president of the United States of America. His integrity and character, more than the brilliance of his intellect, made him the choice of his countrymen as their leader. He loved the peace and tranquillity of his Mount Vernon estate, but when duty called him into the turmoil of public life, he responded. He refused any compensation, expecting the government to pay only his expenses, of which he kept an exact account. He gave forty-five years of his life in the service of his country.

The Prophet Joseph Smith was another great example of integrity. He did not waver from doing as the Lord directed, even at the peril of his life. Following his martyrdom, Elder John Taylor wrote of him: "Joseph Smith, the Prophet and Seer of the Lord, has done more, save Jesus only, for the salvation of men in this world, than any other man that ever lived in it. . . . He lived great, and he died great in the eyes of God and his people." (D&C 135:3.)

President Ezra Taft Benson exemplified sublime integrity.

190

His assignment to Europe by the First Presidency to relieve the sufferings of our Saints after World War II exemplified the nobility of his character.

The Lord expects us to live lives of integrity and to be obedient to his commandments. He said, "Why call ye me, Lord, Lord, and do not the things which I say?" (Luke 6:46), and "Not every one that saith unto me, Lord, Lord, shall enter into the kingdom of heaven; but he that doeth the will of my Father which is in heaven" (Matthew 7:21).

A little lying, a little cheating, or taking a little unfair advantage are not acceptable to the Lord. These are Satan's ways to lead us "carefully down to [destruction]." (2 Nephi 28:8, 21.)

To Saints of the Restoration, the Savior said, "Of him unto whom much is given much is required." (D&C 82:3.) Latter-day Saints have been given much indeed: the gospel of Jesus Christ. That blessing carries a risk. We have been warned, "To him that knoweth to do good, and doeth it not, to him it is sin." (James 4:17.)

Many today trade away their integrity for a very small price. A person who shoplifts a candy bar or makeup or jewelry trades priceless integrity for a meager gain. A person who falsifies a tax return by not reporting income or by claiming invalid deductions compromises valued integrity for a pittance of unpaid income tax. One who avoids paying bills promptly for goods or services received exchanges cherished integrity for a perceived temporary advantage. Husbands or wives who are unfaithful to their spouses trade their prized integrity for a fleeting moment of mirth. Integrity is so precious that it is beyond price; it is invaluable.

The world desperately needs men and women of integrity. Nearly every day we hear of fraud, misapplication of funds, false advertising, or other dealings designed to obtain gain by cheating or deception. The Lord abhors such practices. A proverb states, "A false balance [that is, a deceptive scale] is abomination to the Lord: but a just weight is his delight." (Proverbs 11:1.) The Lord commanded, "If thou borrowest . . . thou shalt restore that which thou hast borrowed." (D&C 136:25.) He commanded the ancient Israelites: "Thou shalt not defraud thy neighbour, neither rob him. . . . Ye shall do no [injustice] in judgment, . . . in weight, or in measure. Just balances, just weights . . . shall ye have." (Leviticus 19:13, 35–36.)

The Israelites were commanded to be more than honest. If they came upon a lost ox, they were to search out the owner so they could return the animal. Today, our intentions and dealings must be similarly pure and sound. If our selfish "hearts are set so much upon the things of this world" (D&C 121:35), we can easily lose our integrity. We must be fair with suppliers, customers, and employees; repay obligations and keep agreements; and never deceive by failing to disclose all facts about an investment or business venture.

We must be honest with the Lord as we pay our tithes. Faithful Saints have learned that he will "open . . . the windows of heaven, and pour . . . out a blessing, that there shall not be room enough to receive it." (Malachi 3:10.) The payment of tithing has less to do with money, but more to do with faith. Let us return one-tenth of our income to the Lord (see D&C 119:4) and never be guilty of robbing him by failing to pay our tithes. We should also remember those in need and contribute generous fast offerings for their assistance.

We show our integrity by caring for and serving others. Let me cite an example.

A young mother of eight children was left without a husband. The oldest child was twelve, the youngest barely one, and one daughter was confined to a wheelchair. This mother moved to a ward that was close to her family and friends. Being single and divorced, she feared that she might be ignored or shunned. However, as she was moving in, ward members streamed in to welcome her, bring food, and offer assistance. She hardly had time to direct those who were unloading the moving van.

After getting settled, she and her family received innumerable expressions of service and love. Her home teachers repaired her appliances and other household items. Her visiting teachers kept very close and made sure she never had to go alone to a church activity. At Christmastime, she found money left anonymously on her porch or received it in a handshake. She received hundreds of dollars toward the purchase of a wheelchair-lift for her van. After being out of town briefly, she returned home and found that ward members had renovated her kitchen.

Her parents, brother, and sisters provided financial and emotional support. They helped take care of her children, accompanied her to the emergency room when a daughter was very ill, built a ramp to the front door for the wheelchair, built shelves for food storage, and helped with yardwork.

All of this kindness lifted her spirits and gave her courage to meet the trials and hardships of each day. Those who looked after her practiced "pure religion" (James 1:27) because of their integrity. Let us "go, and do . . . likewise" (Luke 10:37), as the Savior taught in the parable of the good Samaritan.

The rewards of integrity are immeasurable. One is the indescribable inner peace that comes from knowing we are doing what is right; another is an absence of the guilt and anxiety that accompany sin.

Another reward of integrity is the confidence it can give us in approaching God. When virtue garnishes our thoughts unceasingly, our confidence is strong in the presence of God. (See D&C 121:45.) When we are doing what is right, we will not feel timid and hesitant about seeking divine direction. We will know that the Lord will answer our prayers and help us in our need.

The consummate reward of integrity is the constant companionship of the Holy Ghost. (See D&C 121:46.) The Holy Ghost does not attend us when we do evil, but when we do what is right, he can dwell with us and guide us in all that we do.

Let us live true to the trust the Lord has placed in us. Let us strive for personal, practical integrity in every endeavor, regardless of how mundane or inconsequential it may seem. The small matters accumulate to shape the direction of our lives.

25

THE STRAIGHT AND NARROW WAY

While traveling along a mountainous road one evening through a driving rainstorm punctuated with frequent claps of thunder and flashes of lightning, Sister Wirthlin and I could barely see the road in front of us, on the right, or on the left. I watched the white lines on either side of that road more intently than ever before. Staying within the lines kept us from going onto the shoulder and into the deep canyon on one side and helped us avoid a head-on collision on the other. To wander over either line could have been very dangerous. Then I thought, "Would a right-thinking person deviate to the left or the right of a traffic lane if he knew the result would be fatal? If he valued his mortal life, certainly he would stay between these lines."

That experience of traveling on the mountain road is like life. If we stay within the lines that God has marked, he will protect us, and we can arrive safely at our destination.

The Savior taught this principle when he said: "Enter ye in at the strait gate: for wide is the gate, and broad is the way, that leadeth to destruction, and many there be which go in thereat." (Matthew 7:13.) "For strait is the gate, and narrow the way that leadeth unto the exaltation and continuation of the lives, and few there be that find it." (D&C 132:22.)

King Josiah reigned over Judah in righteousness. When he

was only eight years old, he succeeded his father as king. Scripture tells us that although he was just a boy, he "did that which was right in the sight of the Lord, . . . and turned not aside to the right hand or to the left." (2 Kings 22:2.)

The Lord revealed to the Prophet Joseph Smith: "God doth not walk in crooked paths, neither doth he turn to the right hand nor to the left, neither doth he vary from that which he hath said, therefore his paths are straight, and his course is one eternal round." (D&C 3:2.)

Though these teachings of the Savior are plain and direct, we are still at risk of getting sidetracked. Some people choose to follow the teachings of the Lord and of his living prophet only when it is convenient, rejecting them when sacrifice or deeper commitment is required. Some fail to follow only because the Lord's divine teachings do not agree with their own preconceived notions.

We get sidetracked when we submit to temptations that divert us past the bounds of safety. Satan knows our weaknesses. He puts attractive snares on our paths at just those moments when we are most vulnerable. His intent is to lead us from the way that returns us to our Heavenly Father. Sin may result from activities that begin innocently or that are perfectly legitimate in moderation; but in excess, they can cause us to veer from the straight and narrow path to our destruction.

One example is sports. Many of us enjoy going to ball games and watching them on television. I am no exception. I love to watch a good athletic contest. But if we spend excessive time with sporting events, we may neglect things that are much more important.

Good physical and spiritual health can help us to stay on the straight and narrow way. The Lord gave his code of health in the Word of Wisdom, a "principle with promise" that mod-

196

ern medical science continues to substantiate. (D&C 89:3.) All of God's commandments, including the Word of Wisdom, are spiritual. (See D&C 29:34–35.) We need to nourish ourselves spiritually even more than physically. Are we giving adequate emphasis to our spiritual health?

Another activity that can detract us from the proper way is watching television excessively or viewing improper movies. While fine productions on these media are uplifting and entertaining, we need to be very selective in choosing what we see and how much of our time we devote to such activities. Our precious time must not be diverted to the sideline attractions of vulgar language, immoral conduct, pornography, and violence.

Another temptation to detour us is placing improper emphasis on obtaining material possessions. Jacob, the Book of Mormon prophet, warned: "Do not spend money for that which is of no worth, nor your labor for that which cannot satisfy." (2 Nephi 9:51.) And in even stronger words, he said:

"Because some of you have obtained more abundantly than . . . your brethren ye are lifted up in the pride of your hearts, and wear stiff necks and high heads because of the costliness of your apparel, and persecute your brethren because ye suppose that ye are better than they.

"And now, my brethren, do ye suppose that God justifieth you in this thing? Behold, I say unto you, Nay. But he condemneth you. . . . Do ye not suppose that such things are abominable unto him who created all flesh? And the one being is as precious in his sight as the other." (Jacob 2:13–14, 21.)

The Savior taught clearly the proper value of worldly possessions in his conversation with the rich young ruler who asked what more was required to have eternal life. Having kept all the commandments from his youth, he asked the

Master what he still lacked. Jesus told him to sell all that he had and give to the poor, and come and follow him. But the man went away sorrowing, for he loved his possessions. (See Matthew 19:16–22.) How many of us would pass this test?

Many of us have made sacred covenants to live the laws of sacrifice and consecration. But when the Lord blesses us with riches and affluence, we may give little thought to how we should use these blessings to help build up his church.

The scriptures are full of warnings against worldliness and pride because they too can lead us off course. The Lord explained to the Prophet Joseph Smith that many people veer from the path "because their hearts are set so much upon the things of this world." (D&C 121:35.)

We must also be certain that we do not cross over the lines of safety into paths of immorality. President Ezra Taft Benson declared: "The plaguing sin of this generation is sexual immorality."[1] The broken hearts and broken families that come to my attention demonstrate that immorality is, indeed, a very serious problem in the world and even among some Latter-day Saints.

The first deviation toward moral breakdown in an individual is similar to a spark that ignites a devastating forest fire. On a hot, windy summer day a few years ago in Midway, Utah, embers from a small campground fire were fanned into a raging forest fire that soon swept over the entire mountainside. Before the flames were brought under control, the lives of two outstanding members of the Church were lost. The roaring fire had destroyed the beautiful autumn foliage as well as eighteen homes. We risk similar damage to our moral integrity when we let our guard down for even one brief moment. The spark of an evil thought can enter our mind that could ignite and destroy the moral fiber of our soul.

The Straight and Narrow Way

How can we keep ourselves on the straight and narrow way? The Lord gave the answer over and over again. We must learn the word of God by studying the scriptures, and apply his word by praying to him daily and serving our fellowmen.

Using an apt symbol, the psalmist wrote: "Thy word is a lamp unto my feet, and a light unto my path." (Psalm 119:105.) God's word, then, is the light for our path, the iron rod or railing to which we can cling. It provides the limiting lines that we must not cross if we are to reach our destination.

Through daily study of the scriptures and the words of the modern-day prophets, we can keep our values in line with the will of our Heavenly Father. The scriptures lead us "to the fountain of living waters, or to the tree of life; which waters are a representation of the love of God." (1 Nephi 11:25.)

Daily prayer can help us keep on the path that leads to eternal life. In Proverbs we read: "In all thy ways acknowledge him, and he shall direct thy paths." (Proverbs 3:6.) Praying in private and as families will help us to stay close to our Heavenly Father and to know what is of most value to us and to him. We are very unlikely to stray if we offer a humble, simple prayer at least each morning and evening to express thanks and to seek divine guidance.

As we pray, let us occasionally take a personal inventory to see how we measure up in our righteousness, in meeting the standards of the gospel of Jesus Christ. We each can know for ourselves, as the Lord knows, where we need to improve. We must hold to the standards. If we have advanced in material, outward things, how are we doing inwardly? Are our lives acceptable to the Lord? Are we willing to acknowledge our sins and then make the effort to forsake them, repent, and make the course correction that will return us to the straight and narrow path?

I know that each of us has much to do. Sometimes we feel overwhelmed by the tasks we face. But if we keep our priorities in order, we can accomplish all that we should. We can endure to the end regardless of temptations, problems, and challenges. Those who remain faithful will receive God's greatest blessing—eternal life—and the privilege of living with our Heavenly Father and his Beloved Son in the celestial kingdom.

Elder Marion G. Romney said, "When earth life is over, and things appear in their true perspective, we shall more clearly see . . . that the fruits of the gospel are the only objectives worthy of life's full effort."[2]

The Book of Mormon prophet Jacob declared: "O then, my beloved brethren, come unto the Lord, the Holy One. Remember that his paths are righteous. Behold, the way for man is narrow, but it lieth in a straight course before him, and the keeper of the gate is the Holy One of Israel; and he employeth no servant there." (2 Nephi 9:41.)

I pray that we may enjoy the fruits of the gospel. Let us be faithful and true to our covenants. Let us each be mindful of the straight and narrow way and do all we can to stay within the straight lines in the midst of the storms and temptations of life. Let us study the scriptures, hold to the rod of the word of God, be prayerful in all we do, and perform Christlike acts of service. May we be filled with charity, which is the pure love of Christ, and may that love be reflected in our actions. Then we will observe the "weightier matters" of God's law while not leaving the rest undone. (Matthew 23:23.)

NOTES

1. "Cleansing the Inner Vessel," *Ensign,* May 1986, p. 4.
2. *Conference Report,* October 1949, p. 39.

26

PATIENCE, A KEY TO HAPPINESS

One of the greatest sentences to fall upon human ears comes from the Book of Mormon: "Adam fell that men might be; and men are that they might have joy." (2 Nephi 2:25.) That sentence captures the major possibilities of life. Let me add that we will have genuine joy only as we learn patience.

Patience is defined in such terms as bearing pain or sorrow calmly or without complaint; not being hasty or impetuous; being steadfast despite opposition, difficulty, or adversity.

In a passage from the Book of Mormon, Alma helps us understand patience. After telling about planting a seed that can grow to become a tree, he adds these insightful words: "And behold, as the tree beginneth to grow, . . . if ye nourish it with much care it will get root, and grow up, and bring forth fruit. . . . And because of your diligence and your faith and your patience . . . ye shall pluck the fruit thereof, which is most precious, which is sweet above all that is sweet, . . . and ye shall feast upon this fruit even until ye are filled, that ye hunger not, neither shall ye thirst. . . . Ye shall reap the rewards of your faith, and your diligence, and patience." (Alma 32:37, 42–43.)

I don't know whether we fully appreciate the Book of Mormon, one of our sacred scriptures, as we really should.

One of the clearest explanations of why we need patience to endure the trials of life is set forth by Nephi in these striking words: "For it must needs be, that there is an opposition in all things. If not so, . . . righteousness could not be brought to pass, neither wickedness, neither holiness nor misery, neither good nor bad. Wherefore, all things must needs be a compound in one. . . .

"And if ye shall say there is no law, ye shall also say there is no sin. If ye shall say there is no sin, ye shall also say there is no righteousness. And if there be no righteousness there be no happiness. And if there be no righteousness nor happiness there be no punishment nor misery. And if these things are not there is no God. And if there is no God we are not, neither the earth; for there could have been no creation of things, neither to act nor to be acted upon; wherefore, all things must have vanished away." (2 Nephi 2:11, 13.)

The Apostle Paul gave the purpose of patience in his epistle to the Saints in Rome: "We glory in tribulations . . . knowing that tribulation worketh patience; and patience, experience, and experience, hope." (Romans 5:3–4.)

In 1947, President J. Reuben Clark, Jr., a member of the First Presidency, gave an address entitled "Slipping from Our Old Moorings." He described how we have slipped away from living the Ten Commandments.[1]

If we had slipped away then, where are we nearly fifty years later? In 1947, television and computers were in their infancy. We had no satellite broadcasts, videotapes, no computer fraud. Certainly our moral standards of decency and propriety have slipped from where they were in 1947. Obscenity, nudity, and other forms of pornography that would have made us blush and turn away in shame in 1947 are now thrust at us openly in printed and visual media. They may even be paraded through our homes unless we are careful to keep them out. As a people, we are slipping further from our old moorings today because we are not following our prophets.

A certain amount of impatience may be useful to stimulate and motivate us to action. However, I believe that lack of patience is a major cause of many difficulties and much unhappiness in the world today. Too often we are impatient with ourselves, with our family members and friends, and even with the Lord. We seem to demand what we want right now, regardless of whether we have earned it, whether it is right. Some seek immediate gratification or numbing of every impulse by turning to alcohol and drugs, while others seek instant material wealth through questionable investments or dishonesty, with little or no regard for the consequences. Perhaps the practice of patience is more difficult, yet more necessary, now than at any previous time.

To the Latter-day Saints, the Lord gave patience as one of the divine attributes that qualifies a person for the ministry. (See D&C 4:6.) He counseled them to be patient in their afflictions (see D&C 24:8; 31:9; 54:10; 98:23–24), and to make their decisions in patience (see D&C 107:30). He taught us to be perfect (see Matthew 5:48; 3 Nephi 12:48) and said, "Ye are not able to abide the presence of God now, neither the ministering of angels; wherefore, continue in patience until ye are perfected" (D&C 67:13).

The Lord Jesus Christ is our perfect example of patience. Though absolutely unyielding in adherence to the truth, he exemplified patience repeatedly during his mortal ministry. He was patient with his disciples, including the Twelve, despite their lack of faith and their slowness to recognize and understand his divine mission. He was patient with the multitudes as they pressed about him; with the woman taken in sin; with those who sought his healing power; and with little children. Finally, he remained patient through the sufferings of his mock trials and his crucifixion.

The Apostle Paul, during a ministry of about thirty years between his conversion and his martyrdom in Rome, was flogged five times, beaten severely at least three times, imprisoned several times, shipwrecked three times, and stoned and left for dead on one occasion. (See 2 Corinthians 11:23–27.) Through all of this affliction, he continued his powerful ministry. He wrote to the Romans that God "will render to every man according to his deeds: To them who by patient continuance in well doing seek for glory and honour and immortality, eternal life: but unto them that are contentious [impatient], and do not obey the truth, but obey unrighteousness, indignation and wrath, tribulation and anguish." (Romans 2:6–9.)

The Prophet Joseph Smith's afflictions and sufferings paralleled those of Paul in many respects. Beyond imprisonments, mobbings, and beatings, he suffered the anguish of betrayal by disloyal, unfaithful associates. But he offered the hand of friendship and fellowship to them even after they had opposed and betrayed him.

Some years ago, President Roy A. Welker of the German-Austrian Mission, one of the outstanding mission presidents of the Church, needed to assign a missionary to labor in Salzburg, Austria, to solve a problem in the branch there. Eight new missionaries were soon to arrive in the mission, and he prayed that one of them would have the proper visa and currency to labor in Austria. He continued to pray and waited two weeks for an answer. The night before the eight arrived, the Spirit of the Lord whispered to the president the name of the missionary who should be assigned to Salzburg. The one whose name he received was the one who had the proper credentials to go to Austria. I was that elder.

The president's patience not only helped solve a problem in the branch, but it also blessed me and my family in a way that I never could have foreseen. Shortly after I arrived in Salzburg, that part of the German-Austrian Mission was changed into the Swiss-Austrian Mission. Later, I was transferred to Zurich, Switzerland, where I met Brother Julius Billeter, a warm and friendly member who was a genealogist. He was acquainted with the genealogical records of my progenitors and researched the names of six thousand of my ancestors for whom temple work later was completed.

We should learn to be patient with ourselves. Recognizing our strengths and our weaknesses, we should strive to use good judgment in all of our choices and decisions, make good use of every opportunity, and do our best in every task we undertake. We should not be unduly discouraged or in despair at any time when we are doing the best we can. Rather, we should be satisfied with our progress even though it may come slowly at times.

We should be patient in developing and strengthening our testimonies. Rather than expecting immediate or spectacular manifestations, though they will come when needed, we should pray for a testimony, study the scriptures, follow the counsel of our prophet and other Church leaders, and live the principles of the gospel. Our testimonies then will grow and mature naturally, perhaps imperceptibly at times, until they become driving forces in our lives.

Patience with family members and others who are close to us is vital for us to have happy homes. However, we often seem more willing to be courteous and polite with strangers than with those in our own family circles. Too often criticism, sharp language, and quarreling seem to be acceptable at home but not away from home.

I plead with husbands to be patient with their wives, and with wives to be patient with their husbands. We shouldn't expect perfection; rather, we should look for agreeable ways to work out the differences that arise. Remember President David O. McKay's wise counsel regarding marriage: keep your eyes wide open before marriage and half closed afterward.[2]

Parents need to be patient with their children. They should read to their little children and help them with their schoolwork, even if they have to explain the same thing many times. Elder Richard L. Evans said, "If they [children] find that they can trust us with their trivial questions, they may later trust us with more weighty ones."[3] We must capitalize on their natural curiosity and help them develop a love for learning. We need to teach them the principles of the gospel in simple terms, be patient with them if they disturb family home evening or family prayers, and convey to them the reverence we feel for the gospel, for Church leaders, and for the Savior.

We should also be patient with our youth, especially as they make the transitions from adolescence to adulthood. Many of them have the appearance of adults and think they are adults, but they have had little experience with which to make adult judgments. Let us help them to get the experience they need and to avoid the pitfalls that can harm them.

On the other hand, I urge children to be patient with their parents, even if they seem to be out of touch on such vital issues as dating, clothing styles, modern music, and the use of family cars. Parents have the experience that young people lack. Very few, if any, of the challenges and temptations youth face are new to them. Most important, they love their children and will do anything they can to help them to be truly happy.

I advise all Latter-day Saints to be patient in financial matters. Avoid rash or hurried financial decisions; such decisions require patience and study. Get-rich-quick schemes seldom work. Beware of debt. Be especially careful of easily obtained credit even if the interest is tax deductible. Young couples should not expect to begin their married lives with homes, automobiles, appliances, and conveniences comparable to those their parents have spent years accumulating.

Finally, a word about patience with our Heavenly Father and his plan of eternal progression. How incredibly foolish it is for anyone to be impatient with him, the Father of our spirits, who knows everything and whose work and glory, through his Son, Jesus Christ, is "to bring to pass the immortality and eternal life of man." (Moses 1:39.) As Elder Neal A. Maxwell said, "Patience is tied very closely to faith in our Heavenly Father. Actually, when we are unduly impatient, we are suggesting that we know what is best—better than does God. Or, at least, we are asserting that our timetable is better than his. Either way we are questioning the reality of God's omniscience."[4]

Elder Richard L. Evans said, "There seems to be little evidence that the Creator of the universe was ever in a hurry. Everywhere, on this bounteous and beautiful earth, and to the farthest reaches of the firmament, there is evidence of patient purpose and planning and working and waiting."[5]

Quoting from Elder Marvin J. Ashton: "We do not have to worry about the patience of God, because he is the personification of patience, no matter where we have been, what we have done, or what we, to this moment, have allowed our-selves to think of ourselves. . . . God will not forsake [us]."[6]

I am truly grateful for the Lord's patience with his chil-dren. I am infinitely grateful for his patience with me and for the privilege I have to serve as a special witness of the divinity of Jesus Christ.

I am gratified, as I travel among the members of the Church, to see how many truly live the gospel principles. The Lord has promised: "Those that live shall inherit the earth, and those that die shall rest from all their labors . . . ; and they shall receive a crown in the mansions of my Father, which I have prepared for them. Yea, blessed are they . . . who have obeyed my gospel; for they shall receive for their reward the good things of the earth. . . . And they shall also be crowned with blessings from above." (D&C 59:2–4.)

I pray that we might be patient, especially in adversity, as we meet our challenges of uncertainty, trials, pressure, and tribulation in today's world.

NOTES

1. See *Church News,* March 8, 1947, pp. 1, 8–9.
2. Conference Report, April 1956, p. 9.
3. "I'm Busy. Don't Bother Me Now," *Ensign,* May 1971, p. 12.
4. "Patience," *Ensign,* October 1980, p. 28.
5. Conference Report, October 1952, p. 95.
6. *Speeches of the Year: BYU Devotional Addresses* 1972–73 (Provo, Utah: Brigham Young University Press, 1973), p. 104.

27

PONDERING AND THE SPIRITUAL LIFE

In a revelation given to President Joseph F. Smith is an important message for all of us. "On the third of October," wrote President Smith, "in the year nineteen hundred and eighteen, I sat in my room pondering over the scriptures; and reflecting upon the great atoning sacrifice that was made by the Son of God, for the redemption of the world. . . . As I pondered over these things which are written, the eyes of my understanding were opened, and the Spirit of the Lord rested upon me." (D&C 138:1–2, 11.)

Pondering—which means to weigh mentally, to deliberate, to mediate—can open the spiritual eyes of one's understanding. Also, the Spirit of the Lord may rest upon the ponderer, as described by President Smith.

Jesus admonished the Nephites, "Therefore, go ye unto your homes, and ponder upon the things which I have said, and ask of the Father, in my name, that ye may understand." (3 Nephi 17:3.) We are constantly reminded through the scriptures that we should give the things of God much more than usual superficial consideration. We must ponder them and reach into the very essence of what we are and what we may become.

A story is told about a young builder who had just gone into business for himself. A wealthy friend of his father came to him and said: "To get you started right, I am going to have you build a house for me. Here are the plans. Don't skimp on anything. I want the very finest materials used and flawless workmanship. Forget the cost. Just send me the bills."

The young builder became obsessed with the desire to enrich himself through this generous and unrestricted offer. Instead of employing top-grade labor and buying the finest materials, he shortchanged his benefactor in every way possible. Finally, the last secondhand nail was driven into the last flimsy wall, and the builder handed over the keys and bills, totaling over a hundred thousand dollars, to his father's old friend. That gentleman wrote a check in full for the structure and then handed the keys back to the builder. "The home you have just built, my boy, is my present to you," he said with a pleasant smile. "May you live in it in great happiness!"

In this story, the young builder did not ponder the consequences of his dishonest thoughts and acts. If he had pondered, perhaps he would have come to a clear understanding of what Jesus so long ago described:

"Therefore whosoever heareth these sayings of mine, and doeth them, I will liken him unto a wise man, which built his house upon a rock: And the rain descended, and the floods came, and the winds blew, and beat upon that house; and it fell not: for it was founded upon a rock. And every one that heareth these sayings of mine, and doeth them not, shall be likened unto a foolish man, which built his house upon the sand: And the rain descended, and the floods came, and the winds blew, and beat upon that house; and it fell: and great was the fall of it." (Matthew 7:24–27.) Had he pondered his actions, he might have learned that to consent verbally to do the right thing and then to live and to act without effort to achieve what is right is ruinous.

This story has application for each of us. We must ponder the consequences of our mistakes. Our Father in Heaven has generously given to all of us life, which includes our free agency. With free agency comes the challenge to make the right decisions and choices, including the achievement of joy and happiness. This is an art in itself and must be earned. It is not possible to have a free ride on the road to joy, and there is no real joy that does not involve self-denial and self-discipline; we must ponder our actions and their results.

We know that there is much evil abounding in the world today. Many people are addicted to drugs that cause mental, emotional, and physical problems of great magnitude and long-lasting duration. Many marriage partners are unfaithful, causing the breakup of homes and families. Satan is working harder and is having greater success than perhaps ever before in history.

All evils to which so many become addicted begin in the mind and in the way one thinks. Experience teaches that when the will and imagination are in conflict, the imagination usually wins. What we imagine may defeat our reason and make us slaves to what we taste, see, hear, smell, and feel in the mind's eye. The body is indeed the servant of the mind.

In his widely acclaimed essay "As a Man Thinketh," James Allen reinforced what Jesus so beautifully proclaimed. Mr. Allen wrote: "Man is made or unmade by himself; in the armory of thought he forges the weapons by which he destroys himself; he also fashions the tools with which he builds for himself heavenly mansions of joy and strength and peace. By the right choice and true application of thought, man ascends to the Divine Perfection; by the abuse and wrong application of thought, he descends below the level of the beast. Between these two extremes are all the grades of character, and man is their maker and master. . . . All that a man achieves and all that he fails to achieve is the direct result of his own thoughts."[1]

The insidious process of transforming a person from goodness to evil is a subtle, usually undeliberate one. It is a process of pondering the wrong thoughts, of planting evil seeds in the heart. The word *seeds* is a graphic description of what begins the process and is so well described by Alma:

"Now, we will compare the word unto a seed. Now, if ye give place, that a seed may be planted in your heart, behold, if it be a true seed, or a good seed, if ye do not cast it out by your unbelief, that ye will resist the Spirit of the Lord, behold, it will begin to swell within your breasts; and when you feel these swelling motions, ye will begin to say within yourselves—It must needs be that this is a good seed, or that the word is good, for it beginneth to enlarge my soul; yea, it beginneth to enlighten my understanding, yea, it beginneth to be delicious to me." (Alma 32:28.)

To soundly plant good seeds in one's heart requires prolonged, intense, unremitting pondering. It is a deep, ongoing, regenerating process that refines the soul.

A century ago Stanford University had a most distinguished president, David Starr Jordan. These thoughts from *The Strength of Being Clean* by President Jordan will, I believe, summarize my convictions on this subject: "Vulgarity [now known as pornography] is an expression of arrested development in matters of good taste or good character. . . . Vulgarity weakens the mind, and thus brings all other weakness in its train. . . . It is vulgar to like poor music, to read weak books, to feed on sensational newspapers [or debasing TV], . . . to find amusement in trashy novels, to enjoy vulgar theatres, to find pleasure in cheap jokes, to tolerate coarseness and looseness in any of its myriad forms. . . . [For] the basis of intemperance is the effort to secure through [thoughts first and then] drugs the feeling of happiness when happiness does not exist. Men destroy their nervous system for the tingling pleasures they feel as its structures are torn apart."[2]

Parents should ponder over their family home evenings and their responsibility to teach the gospel to their family. All members should ponder over the instructions received in sacrament and priesthood meetings, in Relief Society, and in messages from home teachers. Priesthood bearers should ponder over their responsibility to honor their priesthood and be examples of righteousness. Quorum leaders should ponder over their quorum members and lead in love and kindness. Young people should ponder over problems that confront them and learn to cope with them in ways that their parents, their leaders, and their Heavenly Father would have them cope so that they might keep themselves clean and pure.

In striving to be the best by God's standards, King Benjamin, a great Book of Mormon prophet, points the way: "But this much I can tell you, that if ye do not watch yourselves, and your thoughts, and your words, and your deeds, and observe the commandments of God, and continue in the faith of what ye have heard concerning the coming of our Lord, even unto the end of your lives, ye must perish. And now, O man, remember, and perish not." (Mosiah 4:30.)

In our quest for pure hearts, may we ponder on righteous acts and thoughts, and may we be faithful and diligent.

Notes

1. New York: Thomas Y. Crowell Co., n. d., pp. 8–9, 34.
2. New York: H. M. Caldwell Co., 1900, pp. 24–25, 27.

28

SEEDS OF RENEWAL

In a hot, dry, desert area of northwest Mexico, farmers plant seeds and grow varieties of corn and beans that are unusually hardy and drought resistant. These varieties survive and flourish in a harsh climate where other plants would wither and die. One of these plants is the white tepary bean. Its seeds will sprout and the plant will grow even when very little rain falls. It sends its roots as deep as six feet into the rocky, sandy earth to find the moisture it needs. It can flower and bear fruit in the 115–degree (Fahrenheit) desert temperatures with only one yearly rainfall. Its foliage remains remarkably green, with little irrigation, even in the heat of mid-July.[1]

Perhaps Latter-day Saints could emulate the example of these hardy, sturdy plants. We should send our roots deep into the soil of the gospel. We should grow, flourish, flower, and bear good fruit in abundance despite the evil, temptation, or criticism we might encounter. We should learn to thrive in the heat of adversity.

Our pioneer ancestors survived and grew stronger in the face of extreme trials and afflictions and made the desert blossom as a rose. My own great-grandfather suffered so much from asthma that he had to walk a mile or two behind the covered wagons crossing the plains to avoid the dust.

However, he always arrived at his destination and did his share of the work.

Our challenges today are different from those of our ancestors. Many of them lived lives of poverty and hardship, while some among us are affluent and complacent. But wealth, abundance, and easy living do not help us develop the ability to flourish when faced with the rigors and reversals of life. Rather than seeking ease, we must plant, cultivate, and nourish within ourselves the seeds that will enable us to withstand the winds and heat of temptation, sin, and evil and help us to live successful, happy, and pure lives. Let us consider a few such seeds.

First, we should plant and nurture the seed of faith in the Lord Jesus Christ, our Savior and Redeemer. We each should develop the faith of Nephi to do the things the Lord has commanded (see 1 Nephi 3:7), knowing that all commandments are given for our good. Nephi expressed his faith in these words: "If it so be that the children of men keep the commandments of God he doth nourish them, and strengthen them, and provide means whereby they can accomplish the things which he has commanded them." When the Lord instructed Nephi to build a ship, his brothers called him a fool to think he could do it. He told them: "If God had commanded me to do all things I could do them. If he should command me that I should say unto this water, be thou earth, it should be earth." (1 Nephi 17:3, 50.)

Next, let us nurture the seed of faith that gives us the courage to follow the prophets. Our prophet today is the Lord's spokesman to mankind at this time. We need the wisdom and the courage to accept his inspired counsel with gratitude and conform our lives to it, because "whether by mine own voice or by the voice of my servants, it is the same."

215

(D&C 1:38.) The revelations given to Joseph Smith on the day the Church was organized apply to Latter-day Saints today: "The church . . . shalt give heed unto all his [the Prophet's] words and commandments which he shall give unto you as he receiveth them, . . . for his word ye shall receive, as if from mine own mouth, in all patience and faith." (D&C 21:4–5.)

Next, we should sow within our hearts the seed of charity, the pure love of Christ. He is the perfect model of charity. His total life, particularly his atoning sacrifice, is a lesson in charity. His every act reflects absolute, unequivocal love for all mankind and for each one of us. His example teaches us that charity means subordinating personal interests willingly and gladly for the good of others. I believe our progress toward exaltation and eternal life depends upon how well we learn and live the principle of charity. Charity must become a fundamental state of mind and heart that guides us in all we do.

We urge home teachers and visiting teachers to look after their families in a spirit of charity. Home teaching and visiting teaching are vehicles for saving souls when they are done the right way with the right intent.

Next, I believe we must constantly nourish the seeds of love, harmony, and unity in our homes and families. Fathers are to preside over their families in kindness. Husbands and wives are to love each other with a pure love that transcends selfishness. In a single-parent family, the parent presides. Parents are to nurture their children and teach them the principles of right living. Regardless of the help other individuals or institutions may give, the Lord has placed this responsibility ultimately with parents. Children are to honor their parents by obeying them, living as they are taught, and fostering peace in the home.

Parents should plant deep into the hearts and habits of

their children the seed of the work ethic. As society has shifted from an agrarian to an urban structure, the joy and necessity of diligent, hard work have been neglected. If our young people do not learn to work while in their parents' homes, they likely will be compelled to learn later in a setting where the lesson may be painful.

The remarks of President J. Reuben Clark Jr. given in 1933 are instructive today. He said: "It is the eternal, inescapable law that growth comes only from work and preparation, whether the growth be material, mental, or spiritual. Work has no substitute."[2]

More recently, Elder Howard W. Hunter counseled: "The first recorded instruction given to Adam after the Fall dealt with the eternal principle of work. The Lord said: 'In the sweat of thy face shalt thou eat bread.' (Gen. 3:19.) Our Heavenly Father loves us so completely that he has given us a commandment to work. This is one of the keys to eternal life. He knows that we will learn more, grow more, achieve more, serve more, and benefit more from a life of industry than from a life of ease."[3]

Parents can plant seeds in the hearts and minds of their children only if they know where their children are and what they are doing. They should not leave the teaching of their children to chance. They should be in charge of their homes and families, remembering that "reproof give[s] wisdom: but a child left to himself bringeth his mother to shame." (Proverbs 29:15.) I have heard of parents who travel extensively for pleasure leaving their teenage children without parental protection for extended periods. Unprotected teenagers can indulge in a "little" sin without realizing the possible consequences in sorrow and disappointment.

Too many young people have the idea that limited sin is

not really wrong because it will be forgiven easily with no consequences. We see some who are guilty of moral sins but are not overly concerned because they expect to repent quickly, thinking all is well. The idea that any sin is unimportant is false; it comes from the devil. "The Lord cannot look upon sin with the least degree of allowance." (D&C 1:31.)

We ask young people who will be approaching marriage within a few years to think of their own unborn children. Think of what these spirits would ask you to do in your life if they could speak to you now.

Parents must know what their children are watching on television. They should set a proper example by watching only those programs that are uplifting and worthwhile, and oppose those that are corrupt and degrading. Many people decry television shows that portray sin and evil as being normal and acceptable, and even preferable to righteous living. However, viewers set the standards for television broadcasting. The networks and stations broadcast the types of programs that viewers want to see. Frank Stanton, a former president of CBS television network, told a Brigham Young University audience that network television standards will continue to decline because they are based on society's standards. He said, "Standards come from the audience . . . ; the audience determines the programming and program content." Further, he said, "I believe there will be more infractions with respect to [immorality] and violence and it will get a lot worse before it gets better because of the changing standards of our society."[4]

What a sad commentary on our society! Again we can learn a great principle from the Book of Mormon. When King Mosiah proposed that judges should rule instead of kings, he said: "It is not common that the voice of the people desireth anything contrary to that which is right; . . . and if the time comes that the voice of the people doth choose iniquity, then is the time that the judgments of God will come upon you." (Mosiah 29:26–27.) That time of iniquity came about sixty years later and at various other times. In the book of Helaman we read that "they who chose evil were more numerous than they who chose good." (Helaman 5:2.) If television viewing choices serve as a valid measure of our society, they who choose evil surely are more numerous than they who choose good.

Finally, I suggest that we plant in our hearts the seed of testimony, a firm unwavering conviction of the truth and divinity of the gospel that we can share freely with power and persuasion. Humble, fervent testimonies borne as prompted by the Spirit can have far-reaching effects.

President Ezra Taft Benson bore such a testimony in October 1959 when he visited the Central Baptist church in Moscow, Russia, and was asked to speak. He described the event later as one of the most moving experiences of his life. The church was filled with about fifteen hundred people seeking to satisfy their spiritual hunger and thirst even though government policy discouraged religion. He testified to them, "God lives, I know that He lives. He is our Father. Jesus Christ, the Redeemer of the World, watches over this earth. . . . Be unafraid, keep His commandments, love one anther, pray for peace and all will be well." In closing, he said, "I leave you my witness as a Church servant for many years that the truth will endure. Time is on the side of truth. God bless you and keep you all the days of your life."

Those present were touched deeply. Many wept openly, including a cynical newsman and a Russian interpreter. The congregation began singing "God Be with You Till We Meet Again," and waved their handkerchiefs in joyous gratitude and in farewell as President Benson and his party left the meeting.[5]

President Benson's testimony made a deep and lasting impression on a minister of the church, Father Alexander. A few years later, this minister told a Finnish member of our church, Sister Irma Airto, that of all the notable people who visited the Baptist church and signed the guest register, Ezra Taft Benson was the greatest. President Benson was visiting Russia as a high official in the United States government, but Father Alexander recognized him as a great spiritual leader. He told Sister Airto, "When you meet Mr. Benson, tell him that we know he is a man of God and I pray for him."

Sister Airto never expected to meet President Benson in person to convey this message. However, when he visited Finland and created the Helsinki Finland Stake in October 1977, she was able to deliver the message, strengthening her testimony that the Lord guides our affairs.

Another example of far-reaching effects of an inspired testimony is that of the prophet Abinadi. The testimony he bore as he called an apostate king, Noah, and his priests to repentance is one of the most significant doctrinal discourses in the Book of Mormon. The king and his priests, except one, rejected Abinadi's teachings and had him put to death. That one was Alma.

Abinadi may have felt that he failed as a missionary because he had only one convert, so far as the record shows. However, that one convert, Alma, and his descendants were spiritual leaders among the Nephites and Lamanites for about three hundred years. His son Alma became the first chief judge of the Nephite people and the high priest over the

Church. Alma's other descendants who became prominent religious leaders include his grandson Helaman; his great-grandson Nephi; and his great-great-great-grandson Nephi, who was the chief disciple of the resurrected Jesus Christ. All of this resulted from Abinadi's lone convert.[6]

I bear my testimony that we can plant in our hearts and minds the seeds I have mentioned, and others. If we will plant them and nurture them, we can be true, faithful, and happy regardless of adversity and the buffetings of Satan.

Notes

1. See Gary Paul Nabhan, "Seeds of Renewal," *World Monitor,* January 1989, pp. 17–20.
2. Conference Report, April 1933, p. 103.
3. "Prepare for Honorable Employment," *Ensign,* November 1975, p. 122.
4. *The Daily Universe,* Brigham Young University, February 1989, p. 1.
5. See Ezra Taft Benson, *Cross Fire: The Eight Years with Eisenhower* (Garden City, New York: Doubleday and Co., 1962), pp. 485–88.
6. See Mosiah 18; also Daniel H. Ludlow, *A Companion to Your Study of the Book of Mormon* (Salt Lake City: Deseret Book Co., 1976), p. 187.

29

A Time of Preparation

There is a beautiful scripture in Ecclesiastes about time: "To every thing there is a season, and a time to every purpose under the heaven.

"A time to be born, and a time to die; a time to plant, and a time to pluck up that which is planted;

"A time to kill, and a time to heal; a time to break down, and a time to build up;

"A time to weep, and a time to laugh; a time to mourn, and a time to dance . . .

"A time to embrace, and a time to refrain from embracing . . .

"A time to keep silence, and a time to speak;

"A time to love, and a time to hate; a time of war, and a time of peace." (Ecclesiastes 3:1–8.)

No matter how old we are, we are always in a state of preparation.

The Savior prepared for his life mission for thirty years. At the age of twelve, he was aware of his mission. When his anxious mother and earthly father sought him three days after the Passover, he asked, "Wist ye not that I must be about my Father's business?" (Luke 2:49.) His ministry lasted only three years, but what he accomplished in those three short years was a miracle and has influenced hundreds of millions of people throughout the world for two centuries.

The purpose of this life is to prepare to meet God. Alma stated this concept so well: "For behold, this life is the time for men to prepare to meet God; yea, behold, the day of this life is the day for men to perform their labors. . . . Do not procrastinate the day of your repentance until the end; for after this day of life, which is given us to prepare for eternity; behold, if we do not improve our time while in this life, then cometh the night of darkness wherein there can be no labor performed." (Alma 34:32–33.)

Prepare and *perform* are the key words in how we will improve our time in this life.

This day is the day to perform our labors. We should not just mark time and kill time, for time is too precious to waste. We do not want procrastination to use up our precious time, for the Lord revealed in that great council in heaven before the foundation of the earth was laid that an earth would be created "whereon these may dwell; and we will prove them herewith, to see if they will do all things whatsoever the Lord their God shall command them; and they who keep their first estate shall be added upon; and they who keep not their first estate shall not have glory in the same kingdom with those who keep their first estate; and they who keep their second estate shall have glory added upon their heads for ever and ever." (Abraham 3:24–26.)

We are told in Jude 1:6 that "angels which kept not their first estate, but left their own habitation, he hath reserved in everlasting chains under darkness unto the judgment of the great day."

We made choices in our first estate, and as a result, we are here today. Today is the time to improve ourselves. We should not procrastinate. Today is the time for us to decide what our priorities will be and how we will accomplish them. Procrastinating decisions that will affect our eternal salvation and seeking for happiness in doing things contrary to the commandments will not help us keep our second estate.

The testing ground of proving ourselves is our day-to-day tasks and responsibilities, such as caring for our physical needs—obtaining food, shelter, and clothing. No doubt the majority of our time is spent in seeking to take care of these basic needs.

Everyone is given the same amount of time. Each of us has twenty-four hours in each day. We all know that some people accomplish several times more than others. There are also some who are over-accelerated, who hurry too much and accomplish too little. Time management is really self-management and discipline in how we manage ourselves in the time allotted. It involves making choices, and choosing how to use that time that is sometimes difficult.

Most people manage their lives by crises. They are driven by external events and circumstances. As each problem arises, they focus on the problem. However, effective time managers are not problem-minded. They are opportunity-minded. They think preventably by using long-range planning. They set their priorities, organize themselves to accomplish these priorities, and then execute their tasks. In other words, they *prepare,* then *perform* their tasks to *improve* on their time.

With so much to accomplish in so little time, how can we manage our day-to-day tasks in a way that all can be accomplished? Here are some suggestions:

1. First, after you have determined your values and priorities, write them down into long-term and short-term goals.

Writing them down will memorialize them. You might use your journal, a planner, or a notebook.

2. Prioritize each goal. One method is to assign the letter "A" to the most important matters; "B," middle important matters; and "C," matters that have little importance. Additional priorities can be assigned to indicate matters that are urgent and those that can wait until tomorrow or next week or month. For example, if an assignment is due tomorrow, complete that one before starting on one that is due next week. If you say yes to something that is urgent but not important, you may also be saying no to something that is more important but less urgent. Each act has an effect on others. Unfortunately, too many people are scheduled to the hilt but actually accomplish little.[1]

3. Another strategy for accomplishing a great deal is to list for each day three items that are both important and urgent. Start with the first one and complete that one before working on the second and third. If you do not complete each item one day, move the uncompleted item or items to the top of the list for the next day.

4. Some items should be of such importance that they are done every day. For example, daily prayers and scripture reading should be at the top of every list. Horace Mann said, "Habit is a cable; we weave a strand of it every day of our life and soon it cannot be broken." Someone once said that if you do something every day consecutively for one month, it will become a habit.

5. Heed the advice found in the Doctrine and Covenants: "Cease to sleep longer than is needful; retire to thy bed early, that ye may not be weary; arise early, that your bodies and your minds may be invigorated." (D&C 88:124.) The early hours of the morning give us a freshness and a time when we

are unencumbered with the cares of the world. It can be a quiet time, a time to become organized and "prepare every needful thing." (D&C 88:119.)

6. Pray for guidance and direction on how to accomplish the tasks before you. "Pray always, that ye may not faint." (D&C 88:126.)

7. "See that all these things are done in wisdom and order; for it is not requisite that a man [or woman] should run faster than he [or she] has strength. And again, it is expedient that he [or she] should be diligent, that thereby he [or she] might win the prize; therefore, all things must be done in order." (Mosiah 4:27.)

8. Take time for physical exercise. One mother with eight children under twelve thought there was no time to spend exercising. However, after joining an aerobics group that met at the ward building each morning, she was surprised at how much better she felt and how much more she accomplished. She was motivated to finish most of her basic housework before leaving for the class, and afterwards the association with other sisters in the ward renewed her spirit to face the rest of the day.

Sister Wirthlin is a great example when it comes to exercising. She either plays tennis or walks two miles every day. She often persuades me to go walking with her, and this is no leisurely stroll. Exercise is an important part of our day, and the time spent in it will pay dividends.

9. Guard well your spare moments. Emerson once said that spare moments are like uncut diamonds. Discard them and their value will never be known. Improve them and they will become the brightest gems in a useful life.

The story is told of a productive writer who travels widely. She always keeps paper and pencil on hand. When others are wishing away the minutes on long flights and agonizing about missed connections, she makes notes for her next book. She has written several novels while waiting for her children at music and dance lessons and sports practices. She loves time. Time is good to her.

What should our priorities be? The Savior taught, "Seek ye first the kingdom of God, and his righteousness; and all these things shall be added unto you." (Matthew 6:33.)

There are three priorities I hope you would consider at the top of your list when making your life choices. Elder Mark E. Petersen, in a *Church News* editorial,[2] mentioned three areas that distinguish our way of life from that of the world:

1. The first way of life that we should follow is to *be clean in everything we do and say.* The scriptures tell us, "Be ye clean, that bear the vessels of the Lord." (Isaiah 52:11.) That means being clean in our dealings with others—no stealing, no deception, no lust or covetousness. It means being clean in our speech, without profanity, filthy stories, slander, or lies; and being clean includes our behavior morally, remembering that the sin of immorality is next to murder. It means being clean in dress and modest. Cleanliness embraces the purity of intent and the avoidance of evil thoughts, which can lead to evil actions.

2. The second way of life is embraced by the second great commandment: "Thou shalt *love thy neighbour as thyself.*" (Matthew 22:39; emphasis added.)

This way is the way of love, understanding, fair dealing, doing unto others as we would want them to do unto us. If we do not love our fellowmen as we love ourselves, we are violating this fundamental commandment. John wrote, "He that loveth not his brother whom he hath seen, how can he love God whom he hath not seen? . . . He who loveth God love his brother also." (1 John 4:2–21.) The Golden Rule is a rule of salvation. Without it, there is no salvation.

Read the Sermon on the Mount. It is filled with fundamentals on human relations. Then read the Beatitudes. Each one is a priceless gem of interpretation of the second great commandment. Our destiny is to become like our Father in Heaven. He has placed us on a testing ground, a field of learning to develop a Godlike character.

Jesus spoke with Mary and Martha about mismanaged priorities. While Mary sat at his feet, learning of salvation, Martha worked in the kitchen. Finally Martha, annoyed that Mary was not helping her, complained to Jesus. He answered her kindly and patiently: "Martha, Martha, thou art careful and troubled about many things, but one thing is needful, and Mary has chosen that good part." (Luke 10:41–42.)

Too often we do not recognize what is needful. We allow what is important in our lives to be replaced by details and activity that we think we are doing for our families. Sometimes these details need to wait so that the words of the Savior may be heard, so that a father can play ball with his son, or so that a mother can take time to talk to her daughter. What is important should receive the most attention in our lives.

In our daily time management, we need to take the time to love our neighbor and develop close and loving relationships with family members. This should be our top priority.

3. Finally, the most important commandment in our way of life is the first great commandment: "Thou shalt *love the Lord thy God with all thy heart, and with all thy soul, and with all thy mind*" (Matthew 22:37; emphasis added)—and, we might add, without reservation. To love God with all our heart is to serve him with all our heart and keep his com-

mandments fully and completely with an eye single to his glory. It is to live a life of worthiness. It is to pay honest tithes and offerings. It is to attend the temple. It is to work on our genealogical records for our dead. It is to hold family home evening with regularity, efficiency, and spirituality. It is to live the Lord's way.

The Savior taught his disciples that if they loved him, they would serve him: "He that hath my commandments and keepeth them, he it is that loveth me." A sure sign of failure to love him is to fail to keep his commandments. The most unhappy people in all the earth are those who have turned bitter against the Church.

In some respects, progressing through life is like running a marathon. We chose to come to this earth and to be tested and proven. How we manage our time will help us to go the distance through this life and prove ourselves to our Heavenly Father.

If we truly seek first the kingdom of God, all things will be added unto us. He will shower blessings upon us beyond our imagination in this life. And then in the great judgment day, we will hear him say: "Well done, thou good and faithful servant: thou hast been faithful over a few things, I will make thee ruler over many things: enter thou into the joy of thy lord." (Matthew 24:25.)

Notes

1. Ideas adapted from Stephen R. Covey and Truman G. Madsen, *Marriage and Family: Gospel Truths* (Salt Lake City: Bookcraft, 1983), pp. 191–93.
2. See Mark E. Petersen, *A Faith to Live By* (Salt Lake City: Bookcraft, 1959), p. 187.

30

"CHOOSE THE RIGHT"

The restored gospel of Jesus Christ powerfully teaches that a loving Father in Heaven has placed us here upon this earth to learn from our experiences, both good and bad. The Lord spoke with tender reassurance to a tortured, disheartened Joseph Smith suffering in the cold, dark dungeon of Liberty jail to remind him: "All these things shall give thee experience, and shall be for thy good." (D&C 122:7.)

In order to make the most of our education, our Father has given us the gift of agency to learn to use wisely during our sojourn on earth. The power to choose, to control our own destiny, was so important that a war in heaven was fought to preserve it. Our Father bore the grief of seeing one-third of his spirit children lost to Satan as casualties of the evil one's determination to destroy the plan of life and exaltation. Our choice to follow the Savior saved us from being cast out and brought us to this mortal probation.

Let us reflect for a moment upon how we have used the tremendous power of agency in our lives thus far. Let us consider the choices we have made. Many of us have chosen to pursue an education or a vocation, a choice that has eternal worth, for the Lord has revealed that "whatever principle of intelligence we attain in this life, it will rise with us in the resurrection." (D&C 130:18.)

"Choose the Right"

President Brigham Young taught that education should "improve our minds and fit us for increased usefulness," and "make us of greater service to the human family."[1] "Education," he explained, "is the power to think clearly, to act well in the world's work, and the power to appreciate life."[2]

To help us graduate successfully from the "college of life," to help us earn some honors in the rigorous curriculum of adult mortality, to help us choose the right when a choice is place before us,[3] may I suggest three simple guidelines. Though simple and familiar, these three principles are eternal and will serve us as well as they have served our ancestors and as they will yet serve our descendants: first, follow Christ; second, follow the Prophet; and third, follow the Spirit.

1. *Follow Christ.*

The Savior lovingly beckons to everyone, to all of our Father's children everywhere throughout all time. His invitation, "Come, follow me," is universally extended to all people across all eras of human history.

> *He marked the path and led the way,*
> *And every point defines*
> *To light and life and endless day*
> *Where God's full presence shines.*[4]

What he declared in the meridian of time stands as unassailably true today as it was nearly two thousand years ago when he proclaimed, "I am the way, the truth, and the life." (John 14:6.) In the Book of Mormon, Jacob powerfully exhorts us to come unto Christ and to follow the Lord's straight course: "O then, my beloved brethren, come unto the Lord, the Holy One, Remember that his paths are righteous. Behold, the way for man is narrow, but it lieth in a straight course before him, and the keeper of the gate is the Holy One of Israel; and he employeth no servant there; and there is none other way save it be by the gate; for he cannot be deceived, for the Lord God is his name." (2 Nephi 9:41.)

Jacob's elder brother, Nephi, queried, "Can we follow Jesus save we shall be willing to keep the commandments?" (2 Nephi 31:10.) The resounding response is found in the Redeemer's own words: "If ye love me, keep my commandments" (John 14:15), "for the works which ye have seen me do that shall ye also do" (3 Nephi 27:21).

To follow Christ, we must obey his commandments.

With all my heart I echo the Savior's admonition that we choose to hear and heed the word of God. "Keep the commandments," we sing. "In this there is safety and peace."[5] In our world today, the only protection from "all the fiery darts of the adversary" (D&C 3:8) is to choose to "put on the whole armour of God, that [we] may be able to stand against the wiles of the devil" (Ephesians 6:11).

And Satan is certainly wily. He is cunning, the master of deception and the father of all lies. Only by keeping *all* the commandments are we protected by "the whole armour of God" from Satan's incessant, insidious efforts to lead us carefully into his power. Peter taught us of Satan's ferocious devotion to our destruction when he wrote to the saints of his day: "Be sober, be vigilant; because your adversary the devil, as a roaring lion, walketh about, seeking whom he may devour." (1 Peter 5:8.)

We must keep *all* the commandments. We cannot approach the gospel as we would a buffet or smorgasbord, choosing here a little and there a little. We must sit down to the whole feast and live the Lord's loving commandments in their fullness.

We who have been taught the commandments know what to do: pray, study the scriptures, fast, pay our tithes and offerings, attend our meetings, partake of the sacrament, magnify our callings, serve others, sustain our Church leaders, do our home teaching and visiting teaching, make and keep sacred covenants, share the gospel, be honest, true, chaste, benevolent, and virtuous.

The righteous King Benjamin, who loved his people dearly, gathered his people together near the end of his righteous life to share with them the deepest feelings of his heart. After reviewing the basic beliefs and commandments of the gospel of Christ with them, he offered this simple but powerful exhortation: "And now, if you *believe* all these things see that ye *do* them." (Mosiah 4:10; emphasis added.)

As we strive to follow the Savior by keeping his commandments, we need to be aware of Satan's powerful persuasive efforts to confound and frustrate the plan of happiness. For example, he would have people believe that chastity and virtue are outmoded traditions of the distant past, that one can indulge in immorality and not suffer the consequences. Such are the lies that he spreads by any and all means possible. In contrast to Satan's deception, ponder the following words from President Spencer W. Kimball, who spoke plainly on this subject:

"That the Church's stand on morality may be understood, we declare firmly and unalterably, it is not an outworn garment, faded, old-fashioned, and threadbare. God is the same yesterday, today, and forever, and his covenants and doctrines are immutable; and when the sun grows cold and the stars no longer shine, the law of chastity will still be basic in God's world and in the Lord's Church. Old values are upheld by the Church not because they are old, but rather because through the ages they have proven to be right. It will *always* be the rule."[6]

No more powerful invitation to follow the Savior can be found in scripture than Moroni's valedictory admonition: "Come unto Christ, and be perfected in him, and deny yourselves of all ungodliness." (Moroni 10:32.) May we follow Christ to a rich, full, abundant life of peace and joy. When we are heavy laden, his promise of soul-refreshing rest is sure. (See Matthew 11:28–29.) And may we follow him to life eternal, to dwell forever with him and with our Father who is in heaven.

In a powerful message entitled "He Invites Us to Follow Him," President Howard W. Hunter explained what it means to follow the Savior: "Christ's supreme sacrifice can find full fruition in our lives only as we accept the invitation to follow him. . . . To follow an individual means to watch him or listen to him closely; to accept his authority, to take him as a leader, and to obey him; to support and advocate his ideas; and to take him as a model. . . . Just as teachings that do not conform to Christ's doctrine are false, so a life that does not conform to Christ's example is misdirected, and may not achieve its high potential destiny."[7]

2. Follow the prophet.

The Savior has declared that whether we receive the word of God "by [his] own voice or by the voice of [his] servants, it is the same." (D&C 1:38.) If we are to follow Christ, we must follow the prophet, the Lord's mouthpiece on earth. The Lord prepared and chose President Howard W. Hunter as the "prophet to guide us in these latter days."[8] May I share a personal experience that taught me a great deal about this Christlike man.

While I was serving as president of the European area of

the Church, Sister Wirthlin and I traveled throughout Finland, Sweden, Denmark, and Norway to hold meetings and conferences with members and missionaries. As we neared the end of our rigorous travels, we arrived, along with President and Sister John Langeland, in the small city of Alta, Norway, where we held a meeting with the members. Afterwards we climbed a beautiful mountain, and at midnight we enjoyed a picnic. It was as light as noonday. At that time of the year, there was no sunset in Alta, which is located near the top of the world, well inside the Arctic Circle. As we watched the sun hover in a straight line as it moved across the horizon, we marveled at the precision and exactness that the Savior employed in creating the earth in all its majesty.

As President Langeland and I reviewed together our many meetings and travels, we were happy that we had made the extra effort to meet with the members in such a remote part of Norway. Over the years, few General Authorities had visited these small and widely scattered branches. But while chatting with the local leaders, we learned that in the city of Hammerfest, on the other side of a high mountain north of Alta, a branch of the Church had been established, a small branch that was not on our itinerary. Hammerfest is one of the world's northernmost cities, making its tiny branch one of the most remote units of the Church.

To our surprise, we learned that in September 1966, Elder Howard W. Hunter, as a member of the Quorum of the Twelve, had been the first General Authority to visit the Hammerfest Branch, a visit that was accomplished with considerable difficulty. The story of that visit as reported in the *Church News* is worth telling because it says so much about the man whom the Lord has now chosen as his prophet, seer, and revelator:

"'Hammerfest is difficult to reach by normal transportation. It was originally planned that the visitors would fly . . . by seaplane. A change in the weather eliminated any possibility of using a plane, as is often the case. It was decided that they should travel by car from Alta, the closest city to Hammerfest with a commercial airport. Snow had started to cover the roads. Several times en route Elder Hunter and Pres. [Leo M.] Jacobsen had to push their car through the snow. When it seemed as if further progress was impossible, a truck came by and towed the car over the summit to Hammerfest.'

"They finally arrived at ten-thirty that night for a meeting that was to have started at seven o'clock, and found that the members had waited for them. 'They had come from a number of places along the north cape and from as far as Kirkenes near the Russian border,' Elder Hunter said."[9] The members in Hammerfest, anxious to meet an apostle of the Lord and to hear the voice of one called as a special witness, waited three and a half hours for Elder Hunter's delayed arrival. Their faith, hope and prayers were rewarded as he shared with them his powerful testimony of the Savior. Despite great hardship, Elder Hunter, with God's blessings and protecting care, kept his commitment to minister to the Lord's sheep in that far-away small branch. "As a result of [his] visit, 'missionaries report[ed] a more friendly attitude among the people of the town and a new feeling of strength among the local members.'"[10]

While impressive and moving, this is not an extraordinary event in the life of President Hunter. Rather, it is quite typical of his wholehearted devotion to the work of the Lord. He has traveled in nearly every corner of the earth. He possesses an indomitable zeal for preaching and proclaiming the gospel. He is undaunted in his determination to encourage the Latter-day Saints to be faithful in obeying God's commandments.

We all remember President Hunter's experience at Brigham Young University when, as he stood up to address a fireside in the Marriott Center, a young man rushed up and threatened him with a bomb. President Hunter did not flinch nor would he read the message demanded by the assailant. The students began to sing "We Thank Thee, O God, for a Prophet," and a group of students and security officers managed to subdue the man. A doctor who came to the podium took President Hunter's pulse following this frightening incident and reported that it was normal. He resumed his speech by saying, "Life has a fair number of challenges in it." He stopped, looked over the audience, and added, "as demonstrated."[11] This is another good example of a man with a purpose who was not distracted from his sacred calling regardless of danger.

President Hunter has asked us all to "live with ever more attention to the life and example of our Lord, Jesus Christ, especially the love and hope and compassion He displayed." He wants us "to treat each other with more kindness, more courtesy, more humility and patience and forgiveness."[12] In short, he asks us to develop and demonstrate Christlike attributes in all our dealings with others—to love our neighbors as ourselves. To show compassion, we must possess charity, "the pure love of Christ" that the Father bestows upon "all who are followers of his Son, Jesus Christ." (Moroni 7:46–47.)

In recent years the Church has rushed humanitarian aid to flood victims and to refugees fleeing oppressive conditions and famine in many parts of the world. As a church, we are working to heed our prophet's counsel to show Christlike compassion toward our neighbors throughout the earth. But what are we doing individually to follow the prophet's call to provide compassionate service to our fellow beings?

President Hunter has also asked us "to establish the temple of the Lord as the great symbol of [our] membership and the supernal setting of [our] most sacred covenants," and encouraged us to draw closer to the Savior as "a temple-attending and a temple-loving people." "Let us hasten to the temple," he has said, "as frequently as time and means and personal circumstances allow."[13]

I hope that those who are of age and are eligible to do so will take time to attend the temple regularly. Even if a temple is not close by, each individual should work to become and remain temple worthy. President Hunter has said that it is the "deepest desire of [his] heart to have every member of the Church temple worthy."

Just as we must seek a healthy balance in our temple attendance, we must also see that "all . . . things are done in wisdom and order" (Mosiah 4:27) in regard to our gospel study, and especially in regard to hearing and heeding the counsel of our prophet and of the others whom the Lord has called to lead the Church. Let us not grow so busy in our daily activities that we thoughtlessly fail to "feast upon the words of Christ." (2 Nephi 32:3.)

3. *Follow the Spirit.*

All who teach in the Church should teach by the power of the Spirit. We have been instructed that "if [we] receive not the Spirit [we] shall not teach." (D&C 41:14.) The prophet Nephi testified that the Holy Ghost "will show unto [us] all things what [we] should do." (2 Nephi 32:5.) Let us follow the Spirit and heed its quiet promptings. Learning to follow the Spirit requires considerable effort and ongoing attention.

Recently I was reminded of how vital it is to always be alert to the quiet whispering of the Holy Ghost. While on an assignment in Hawaii, Sister Wirthlin and I visited the island of Molokai, where one of the world's few remaining leper colonies is found. We drove into the mountains to a trail that leads to an overlook, and from there the colony can be seen in the distance below. After laboring up the trail, we were disappointed to discover that rain and fog obscured the valley below us and we could not see the colony. As we walked back to our car, we passed a young man headed toward the overlook. I offered a polite greeting, and from his answer, I could tell that he was from Germany.

I served a German-speaking mission in Austria and Switzerland as a young man. Here was a young man whose countenance bespoke a sincere heart and an approachable personality, and I spoke his language and understood his culture. I felt prompted to open my mouth and introduce the gospel to him, but because other people were around us, our brief encounter was interrupted, and we went our separate ways without my having said a word about the restored gospel of Jesus Christ. I failed to be the missionary that every member of the Savior's church ought to be.

As we drove away, I had the disturbing feeling that I had failed in my duty to proclaim the gospel. I remembered the Lord's words in the Doctrine and Covenants: "But with some I am not well pleased, for they will not open their mouths, but they hide the talent which I have given unto them, because of the fear of man. Wo unto such, for mine anger is kindled against them." (D&C 60:2.)

We drove around the island to see Molokai's beautiful waterfalls. After many miles, the road came to a dead-end, and we got out of our car to enjoy the beautiful surroundings. We had been there only a few moments when another car drove up and stopped. The young man we had seen on the overlook trail got out of the car, smiled, and gave me a warm handshake. As I grasped his outstretched hand, I thought to myself, *This time I will do my duty!*

We introduced ourselves, and I learned that he attended a university in a small city south of Dusseldorf, Germany. I spoke of my experiences in his country and of my admiration for the German people. Speaking of my work in Europe gave me an opportunity to explain some of the basics of the gospel. As we parted, I asked for his address and telephone number, which he gladly shared with me. I felt that he was truly a newfound friend and an interested investigator.

Upon my return to Salt Lake City, I wrote to the president of the Germany Dusseldorf Mission. I explained how Sister Wirthlin and I had met this outstanding young man and gave him his address, asking him to send missionaries to continue the gospel discussion that I had begun in Hawaii.

I don't believe it was happenstance that my wife and I met this young man twice. Our meetings were not chance encounters or mere coincidence. But the Lord doesn't always give us a second chance to share the gospel. I had failed to follow the Spirit the first time when the still small voice spoke to my heart and mind to prod me to action. But when I saw that young man get out of his car later, I quickly made up my mind I would not fail a second time and that I would open my mouth as the Lord so emphatically commands in revelations that apply to all of us.

In the thirty-third section of the *Doctrine and Covenants,* the Lord commands us three times in three verses to "open our mouths": "Open your mouths and they shall be filled, and you shall become even as Nephi of old . . . Yea, open your mouths and spare not, and you shall be laden with sheaves upon your backs, for lo, I am with you. Yea, open your mouths and they shall be filled, saying: Repent, repent, and prepare ye the way of the Lord, and make his paths straight; for the kingdom of heaven is at hand." (D&C 33:8–10.)

In the first section of the Doctrine and Covenants, the Lord reveals that one of the principal purposes of the restoration is to proclaim the gospel—to bring truth and priesthood authority back to the earth so that missionary work can be organized and carried out as a mighty effort upon the earth in the last days. In verse 23, he explains that one of the reasons he called Joseph Smith to his prophetic work was so that "the fullness of [the] gospel might be proclaimed by the weak and the simple unto the ends of the world, and before kings and rulers."

Each of us has the sacred responsibility to proclaim the gospel. The Savior's commandment applies to all members of the Church, not just to full-time missionaries or to returned missionaries. We each have the responsibility to follow the Spirit when it prompts us to share the gospel so that others can come to follow the Savior.

We must act when the Spirit speaks! When I hearkened to the Spirit, the young man from Germany responded positively to my message. But it wasn't really *my* message. It was God's message, brought to my mind by the Spirit of the Lord. I was but an instrument in the Lord's hands, led by his Spirit to open my mouth and proclaim the message of the Restoration. In opening my mouth, I became, as the Lord promises, "even as Nephi of old." (D&C 33:8.) Father Lehi gives this explanation of why his son was so adamant in proclaiming the gospel: "Behold, it was not [Nephi], but it was the Spirit of the Lord which was in him, which opened his mouth to utterance that he could not shut it." (2 Nephi 1:27.)

The Spirit will always guide and direct aright. It will protect us from temptation, enlighten our minds, and comfort our hearts. The Lord has told us: "Put your trust in that Spirit which leadeth to do good—yea, to do justly, to walk humbly, to judge righteously; and this is my Spirit." He then goes on to promise: "I will impart unto you of my Spirit, which shall enlighten your mind, which shall fill your soul with joy; and then shall ye know, or by this shall you know, all things whatsoever you desire of me, which are pertaining unto things of righteousness, in faith believing in me that you shall receive." (D&C 11:12–14.)

The Holy Ghost will keep us ever vigilant, for, as Alma taught, Satan desires to have us, "to sift [us] as chaff before the wind." (Alma 37:15.) We need to listen to the still small voice and "suffer not [ourselves] to be led away by any vain or foolish thing." (Alma 39:11) We need to focus our energies on the things that matter and not waste our lives laying "up for [ourselves] treasures upon the earth where moth and rust doth corrupt." (Matthew 6:19; 3 Nephi 13:19.) Let us not trade away our eternal spiritual birthright for a mess of materialistic pottage.

When I was called to serve and sustained as a member of the Council of the Twelve Apostles in October 1986, I shared some fundamental feelings of my heart that the Spirit brought to my mind. On that occasion, greatly humbled by the sacred trust the Lord and his prophet, President Ezra Taft Benson, had placed upon me, I expressed these thoughts:

"Our religion is really the only thing we will have left ultimately and we must love it dearly. The gospel of Jesus Christ is more enduring than fame, more precious than riches, more to be desired than happiness. Understanding and living the gospel leads to the possession of a Christ-like character. The aim of each of us is to live a noble and exemplary life.

"Our Heavenly Father has endowed us with hearts of

242

courage and faith, with strong wills, and with the ability to understand and to see clearly the difference between right and wrong. He has mercifully clothed us, each member, with the gift of the Holy Ghost, which gives us insight and personal power. . . . The light that emanates from our Savior beckons us on, undismayed. A righteous self-discipline can and will rule our lives."[14]

The truths of the gospel do not change. These words ring just as true today as when I first spoke them. If we will follow Christ, follow his prophet, and follow his Spirit, we will always choose the right. And, as a result of our wise choices, our testimony of our Heavenly Father's plan and purpose for our lives will grow stronger, and great blessings of joy, happiness, and peace will be ours.

NOTES

1. *Discourses of Brigham Young,* p. 255.
2. As quoted by LeGrand Richards, *A Marvelous Work and a Wonder* (Salt Lake City: Deseret Book, 1976), p. 384.
3. "Choose the Right," *Hymns,* no. 239.
4. *Hymns,* no. 195.
5. *Hymns,* no. 303.
6. *Ensign,* November 1980, p. 96 (emphasis added).
7. *Ensign,* September 1994, p. 2.
8. *Hymns,* no. 19.
9. Eleanor Knowles, *Howard W. Hunter* (Salt Lake City: Deseret Book, 1994), pp. 175–76.
10. Ibid., p. 176.
11. Ibid., pp. 305–6.
12. Statement to the Press, June 6, 1994.
13. Ibid.
14. *Ensign,* November 1986, pp. 60–61.

INDEX

245

Index

Desire, 86, 98–99
Dikes, 47–48
Diogenes, 138–39
Drucker, Peter, 60
Duty, 32–33, 92–95

Education, 230–31
Enduring to the end, 153, 167–68
Enoch, city of, 7, 186
Entertainment: undesirable, 17–18, 67–68, 134, 142–43, 212–13, 218; excessive attention to, 196–97
Evans, Richard L., 62, 130–31, 206, 207
Evil: small acts of, 15–16, 66–68, 191; prevalence of, in our day, 23, 52, 78, 129, 211; tenacity of, 34; role of thoughts in, 211–12; chosen by voice of people, 219
Exaltation, striving for, 72–73
Example: setting, 76–77, 94, 99–100; of Savior, 128–29; of parents, 131; in missionary work, 134–35; as great inheritance, 139
Exercise, 226

Faith, 54, 105; in Christ, building testimony on, 126–28; principles of, 171–72; role of patience in, 207; nourishing seeds of, 215–16
False doctrine, 121
Families: Satan's attack on, 52; righteous, importance of, 52–53; building spiritual strength in, 53, 216–17; kindness in, 131–32; patience in, 205–7
Family home evening, 55–56
Fasting, 33–34
Fellowshipping, 82–83, 87–91
Finances: contributing, story of,

80–82; patience in matters of, 207
Football game, 62–64
Forest fire, analogy of, 198
Forgiveness, 9–10, 109
Fraud, 183–84, 191–92

Garfield, James A., 144–45
Gibbons, Francis M., 163
Goals, 148–49, 224–25
God the Father: coming to know, 27; nature of, 40, 116, 171; potential to become like, 65; building relationship with, 65–70; Joseph Smith's faith in, 105; will of, 170–72, 178; being patient with, 207; loving, is first commandment, 228–29
Godhead, 40–41
Goethe, 137
Good and evil: knowledge of, 6, 118–19, 187–88; division between, 12–13; worldly confusion of, 18; drama of human struggle with, 31; choosing between, 130–31, 152
Gospel: major principles of, 40–45, 116; holds answers to world's problems, 78; teaching, to less–active families, 89–90; accepting, 96; counsel to teachers of, 121; restored through Joseph Smith, 139–40
Government: seeking wise leaders in, 134; ideals of, 138
Grant, Heber J., 120
Guile, being without, 180–86

Habit, 225
Halamandaris, Val and Bill, 19–20
Hale, Edward Everett, 33
Happiness, 92–93, 133–34

Index

Index

Index